P9-EMR-377

(Continued)

Crossing the Digital Divide

RACE, WRITING, AND TECHNOLOGY IN THE CLASSROOM

Barbara Monroe

Foreword by Victor Villanueva

Teachers College, Columbia University
New York and London

Published by Teachers College Press, 1234 Amsterdam Avenue, New York, NY 10027

Library of Congress Cataloging-in-Publication Data

Monroe, Barbara Jean, 1948–
    Crossing the digital divide : race, writing, and technology in the classroom / Barbara Monroe ; foreword by Victor Villanueva.
        p.   cm. — (Language and literacy series)
    Includes bibliographical references (p.   ) and index.
    ISBN 0-8077-4463-8 (cloth: alk. paper) — ISBN 0-8077-4462-X (pbk. : alk. paper)
    1. English language—Composition and exercises—Study and teaching—United States. 2. English language—Composition and exercises—Study and teaching—Data processing. 3. English language—Rhetoric—Study and teaching—Data processing. 4. English language—Rhetoric—Study and teaching—United States. 5. English language—Rhetoric—Computer-assisted instruction. 6. Report writing—Study and teaching—Data processing. 7. Report writing—Computer-assisted instruction. 8. Educational technology—United States. 9. African Americans—Education. 10. Word processing in education. I. Title. II. Language and literacy series (New York, N.Y.)

PE1405.U6M66   2004
808'.042'071073—dc22   2003068697

ISBN 0-8077-4462-X (paper)
ISBN 0-8077-4463-8 (cloth)

Printed on acid-free paper
Manufactured in the United States of America

11   10   09   08   07   06   05   04   8   7   6   5   4   3   2   1

For my daughter Ruth, who taught me
the meaning of ruth

Contents

Foreword

1967. I'm 18 years old, no diploma, somehow working for U.S. Accountants Computer Systems. I operate a 16K Honeywell H-200 computer. It takes up a large, windowless, temperature-controlled room: punch-card reader, paper-tape reader, four reel-to-reel tape drives, a printer about the size of a large desk. I help to generate accounting sheets—accounts payable, accounts receivable—kind of like a giant computer-generated checkbook tally for Los Angeles businesses. The computer generated the data. It was a data processor.

1969. I'm a company clerk in Vietnam, behind a portable manual typewriter.

1983. A friend lets me borrow his "portable" Kaypro, about the size of a small suitcase, metal, a 4-inch or so monitor. It looks like something from a 1950s sci-fi movie. It's a glorified typewriter, saving me from the gyrations I would go through to make a corrected page fit within the scheme of pages. (I find a gross error on page 5 of an eight-page paper, say. I have to retype, but I don't want to retype the last four pages, so I work at retyping in such a way as to get page 5 to end in such a way as to move seamlessly onto the already-typed page 6—very time consuming way to save time.) Rather than a data processor, the computer functioned for me solely as a word processor.

1991. Fellow faculty members within the department and a few others begin communicating over e-mail after all kinds of glitches. But the computer is now becoming more and more a communication device, more than a processor, a rhetorical tool.

1994. I discover the World Wide Web. And suddenly communications take on large connotations; discourse itself takes on large connotations, as rhetoric puts other symbol systems, not just alphabetic literacy, at my disposal.

1998. The Literacy Crisis is suddenly an anachronism. It's now a Digital Divide. And it's being discussed in terms of "access."

As I heard and read about the digital divide, I found myself troubled by the question of "access." I had had access to banks always, but for quite a while, I had no money with which to take advantage of that access. I worried that a computer would no more be the answer to inequity than literacy alone had been, or the typewriter, or the television. More than just more computers had to be at play. But too often the response to something more than computers was "culture," in very predictable ways—some cultures took to the computer while other cultures didn't. That seemed to suggest that different values were at play. It was an old story, saying that Mexican Americans, for instance, didn't value higher education, when the issues were much more economic than moral. But cultural discussions tended to ignore the economic. So when it came to the digital divide, it seemed, it felt, like the discussion turned either to the purely economic—access—or to the purely cultural.

But we know that to speak of technology is always to speak of value systems and economic systems tied intricately together. We have even developed a way of talking about the world in these terms. Those who haven't access to technologies of various sorts are placed lower down the hierarchy of values that represent real economies—they are Third World peoples. We even place a value system on particular technologies—literacy versus the apparently oral technology of television (apparently oral, since most of what is on TV is scripted), with the PC as somehow in the fray. Questions turn to hidden discussions of wasted money versus well-spent money, to the values of those needing access. Will students use the PC as a modified TV, wasting resources? Or will the PC gain students access to the technology we seem no longer to recognize as one—literacy? PC as TV or video game is clearly lower on our value system than PC as means to literacy.

Literacy: lines drawn in particular ways on wax or slate or skin or papyrus to represent the sounds that represent things and ideas. Although I'm not claiming superiority, alphabetic literacy was a great invention, what with relatively few graphic symbols that could be used to represent all the sound systems of a language. Alphabetic literacy had a democratizing potential. No great amounts of leisure were necessary to master a few dozen graphic symbols and the sounds they represented. Despite its potential, it was denied to many over time; and not all who mastered literacy could transcend poverty and menial labor.

The great literacy machine of the nineteenth century—the typewriter—offered to help change the perception of women in the workplace. Women could make their social and industrial value known. And women could earn. But that instrument ultimately became a means of chaining women to the machine. Young women sent to detention homes and camps received the same training as young women in fine middle-class schools—secretarial training. When *secretary* equates with real power, it is still a male-dominated, male-associated term—Secretary of State or Secretary of Defense. A technical advance, a value, an economy.

Today the technical advance is the PC, and some in the Third World within the First World—those residing in ghettos, slums, and rural areas, which include the American Indian reservations—seek to acquire this potentially democratizing, potentially liberating tool. But Barbara Monroe tells us that the other side of the digital divide can be just another place for menial labor behind a keyboard—or it can be a new, liberating space.

There is nothing inherently, essentially wonderful about technology, after all. Crossing the digital divide tends to mean that the machines will be available. It's as if the machines by their very presence would transform problems of literacy, poverty, powerlessness, and cultural isolation and ignorance (a mutual cultural ignorance between those believing themselves to have power and those knowing they haven't). Barbara exposes this essentialist notion of technology, demonstrating in powerful ways that access alone isn't at issue. She complicates notions of technology so that the television no less than the computer becomes a means to gaining the fundamental technology of our society-at-large: literacy.

While Barbara causes us to rethink essentialized notions of technology, she risks essentializing cultural identities. But hers is a strategic essentializing (to borrow from Gayatri Spivak). She describes the cultural ways with words of poor African American students of Detroit, poor Latino and Latina students, Filipino and Filipina students, and American Indian students of the Pacific Northwest so that teachers might be reminded that the learning needs to be mutual if the computer is to liberate rather than enchain. Barbara makes it clear that we cannot be simply imparters of even this knowledge—these machines that we may have had at our fingertips for as long as decades but which may be completely new to our students. These machines are tied to their users, not value-free, not culture-free. We have the potential to force students to submit (which would also mean to resist). And we have the potential to entice students into engaging in real dialogue—linguistically rich, culturally, ideologically, economically rich dialogue. In the pages that follow, Barbara walks us through technology, computer technology, and ways of crossing the digital divide that are value rich. In the pages that follow, she shows us ways that have the potential, in her words, "to create a critical pedagogy for the electronic age."

Victor Villanueva
Washington State University

Acknowledgments

I have many people to thank for this endeavor. The two projects discussed in Chapter 2 on Detroit and Chapter 4 on Rondo (a pseudonym) would not have happened without generous funding. The Detroit project was funded by Detroit Public Schools and by the Kellogg Foundation through the office of Doug Van Houwelling, then Vice Provost for Information Technology at the University of Michigan. The Rondo paper-collection project was funded by a federal grant entitled CO-TEACH, an acronym for Collaboration on Teacher Education Accountable to Children with High-Needs. CO-TEACH funded the collection of papers, as well as a computer lab, travel, release time, and a research assistant. For this support, I owe a debt of gratitude to the coprincipal investigators of CO-TEACH—Tariq Akmal, Dawn Shinew, Gerald Maring, Merrill Oaks, and Michael Pavel—as well as the CO-TEACH project administrator, Mea Moore.

The project at Rondo involved many individuals who played important roles, however mundane. Neal "The Scan Man" Endacott, Lynn Gordon, and Karen Weathermon all assisted in scanning, transcribing, and proofreading the papers from Rondo. Most especially, I will always be grateful to Lorraine Scrimgeour, the teacher; her students, who so enthusiastically embraced the project; Mitzi Gilbert, the teacher who brought Lorraine and me together; and Kelly Garza, the principal who gave us his wholehearted support.

For the Detroit project, many people helped in myriad ways: attending meetings, making site visits, offering policy advice, writing letters of support, suggesting implementation models, conducting professional development workshops, enlisting and training tutors, setting up e-mail accounts, networking computers, troubleshooting networks, and ordering pizza. All of my colleagues at the English Composition Board, the former writing program at the University of Michigan, were somehow involved with the project at various stages over five years: Jay Robinson, Bill Condon, Wayne Butler, Rebecca Rickly, Emily Lardner, Helen Fox, Becky Reed Rosenberg, Barbra Morris, LeeAnn Sutherland, Colleen LaPere, and George Cooper.

Thank you, George, for codirecting the project with me the year of its official launch. I want to acknowledge the many people at the Detroit high school who worked to make this project possible, but especially Sallie Polk, the principal, and Jackie Graham, the classroom teacher who connected her students with George's and mine. However, the two people most responsible for getting this project off the ground were Michael Smith and Lu Jennings. Michael, the information technology specialist for the district, worked the hardest and longest of everyone in Detroit or Ann Arbor in getting the school online. Lu Jennings, a longtime resident of Detroit and a very spiritual person whose inner light always shines bright, first invited me to the school and then continued to open doors that are generally shut to outsiders. Thank you all.

I am also grateful to Karen Maguigad, a former master's degree student of mine and the teacher who allowed me access to the transcript of her interschool threaded discussion on which Chapter 3 is based. Both Karen and her teacher-collaborator at the tribal school, Teresa Scofield, demonstrated a Freirean courage to teach, and I am indebted to both. Through her project, Karen taught me far more than I taught her: As Freire said, "Those who teach, learn."

I also want to thank a host of readers who offered thoughtful and constructive suggestions at various stages in this book's progress: Debbie Lee, Phyllis Frus, Becky Reed Rosenberg, Cindy Wambeam, Karen Weathermon, Merry Farrington, and Bill Condon, as well as the blind reviewers and editors at Teachers College Press. I took all their suggestions to heart, as should be evident in the book's published version.

In so many ways, this book bears the marks of my three mentors. Each has deeply informed my thinking on literature, instructional technology, and composition, respectively. I have Warwick Wadlington to thank for my abiding interest in literary expressions of Southern culture and the African American rhetorical tradition. To John Slatin, I owe a debt of gratitude for introducing me to the instructional possibilities of computers; too, our conversations through the years were really first brainstorming sessions of the case studies in this book. But Bill Condon has been the one person most responsible for putting me on my professional path. His longstanding support of my work started at the University of Michigan and continues today at Washington State University. Thank you for everything, Bill.

The names of schools, student writers, and family and friends that students mentioned in their work are all pseudonyms, to protect their anonymity. I want to thank all of them, as well as their brave teachers, for inspiring me to get their words out into the world.

And finally, I thank my daughter Ruth, who sacrificed much of our mother-daughter time together over the past decade, as I made time to work with schools and to write this book.

Introduction

In *Technology and Literacy in the Twenty-First Century: The Importance of Paying Attention* (1999), Cynthia Selfe urges English educators at all levels to strive for critical technological literacy in their respective classrooms. This kind of literacy education, she maintains, must spring "from an understanding of the local and particular," and further, "suggestions for a critical engagement . . . must allow for wide variations in social, political, economic, and ideological goals, as well as wide variations in teachers, students, administrators, citizens, and communities" (p. 148).

This book responds specifically to Selfe's call, paying attention to "the local and particular" as it examines the discursive practices—both online and off—of students of color. Not coincidentally, they attend high-poverty schools, linguistically isolated from the mainstream. As these schools come online, educators and researchers have increased access to communities where nonwhite discursive practices and interaction styles prevail. These indigenous rhetorics, I argue, are culturally marked. These are the rhetorics that secondary school students of color bring with them to school, and these are the rhetorics that they bring with them online. By framing this investigation on race, writing, and technology in terms of the local and particular, this book both raises and revisits several issues in literacy education for students of color. Most of these issues revolve around reconciling writing theory and pedagogy with nonwhite, indigenous rhetorics. As communities on the other side of the digital divide become immersed in electronic media, the impact of technology on the lives, literacies, and learning of students of color must also be taken into account.

My primary focus is what has been variously termed *contrastive rhetoric* (Kaplan, 1966) and *alternative discourses* (Schroeder, Fox, & Bizzell, 2002). Contrastive rhetoricians tend to focus on culturally marked organizing principles in the college writing of international students who write English as a Second Language (ESL). This book, however, trains its sights on American secondary school students of color whose first language may or may not be English. I also more broadly construct the subject of alterna-

1

tive discourses to include both the forms and norms that define the linguistic behaviors, interaction styles, and learning preferences of a discursive community. Different chapters feature different technologies: e-mail, Web-based threaded discussions, and movies and television, with passing mention of chat and computer games.

After a chapter that contextualizes the public policy debate on access, three case studies offer snapshots of four different schools as they enter the Information Age. One chapter focuses on the writings, both over e-mail and on paper, of African American high school students in Detroit; another examines an online discussion between a tribal school and a predominately Latino high school; and a third analyzes the cultural distinctions in written storytelling practices of seventh graders at a multiracial school on a large, remote Indian reservation. Each of these three chapters goes on to explore the implications of its ethnographic findings for writing teachers at all levels, whether they teach at high-poverty schools or not. The closing chapter revisits the access issue, arguing that high-poverty schools do not usually have student access, and when they do, computers are used to reform, rather than transform, schooling.

Chapter 1, "Reconsidering the Terms of the Debate," aims to retool the debate on universal access and its most popular metaphor, the digital divide, by analyzing the origins of the metaphor and the other rhetorical divides it has spawned in the public debate on access in the 1990s and early 2000s. The metaphor itself narrowly confines the terms of the debate to oppositional binaries, thereby foreclosing the options for addressing systemic inequities for which the access issue is merely symptomatic. Notably, dualisms with their hidden hierarchies have always come at the expense of the "have-nots," largely for the simple reason that the terms of the debate were, and continue to be, defined by the "haves." Reconstructing the divide, this time from the perspective of the "have-nots," should help surface some of the complications that come with access, variously defined. Restoring this complexity to the debate is prerequisite to reconsidering how and to what effect computers should be used in public school instruction.

Chapter 2, "Putting One's Business on Front Street," examines e-mail exchanges between students at a Detroit high school and writing tutors at the University of Michigan. These electronic interactions entailed sharing personal information, either in one-to-one conversations or in assigned writing. Because etiquette governing information sharing and personal disclosure differs across race and gender lines, the project quickly became a study in cross-cultural communication. The Detroit students were keenly aware of what kind of "business" they put on "Front Street" and sought to control that information—and the public image of themselves and of their school—largely by handling language in culturally specific ways. Consistently, the Detroit students code-shifted from African American English to Edited American English, but their writing nonetheless retained features of stylistic registers valued in African American expressive culture.

I contend that these code and style shifts were sensitive to the proximal distance of readers, the perception of readers' knowledge of African American English, and the social domains of school and church (as opposed to the playground and the street). This case study exposes the many ideological conflicts inherent in teaching writing to African American teenagers, whose linguistic behaviors are further complicated by gender differences. Although no easy task, I maintain that the demands of "good writing" with its assumptions about self-expression and information sharing in public domains can be negotiated with the signature strengths of the African American rhetorical tradition.

Chapter 3, "Crucible for Critical Literacy," analyzes the transcript of an extended threaded discussion on Arthur Miller's *The Crucible* between two schools from different communities with opposing political views and histories: one, a Latino-majority school; the other, a tribal school. This case study clearly demonstrates that the "have-nots" are not a monolithic mass, as portrayed in the national debate on access, for it captures the culturally distinctive ways that students of Mexican descent and Plateau Indian students interact and negotiate conflicts among themselves and with outsiders. This chapter makes the case that students are fully capable of teaching one another critical literacy. Ironically, the sheer number of postings in a multiclass online discussion actually militates against critical engagement. I go on to suggest one way that teachers who are working with huge class sizes and limited access, might both frame and follow up online discussion in the physical context of the face-to-face class in order to critically engage students in the local issues that shape their lives.

The case study discussed in Chapter 4, "Storytime on the Reservation," does not examine electronic transcripts, as do the other two case studies, although the e-mail contact between the teacher and me, as a researcher, sustained the project that made this case study possible. Based on papers collected via postal mail, this investigation looks at fictional narratives written by seventh graders at a multiracial reservation school, where students of Mexican descent and Plateau Indian students together constitute the majority, and whites and Filipinos, the minority. Culturally distinct discursive practices emerged in several assignments asking for different kinds of narrative, as my analysis of one such assignment illustrates. What I call the *discourse of reserve* characterized the stories of Latino students; oral performance cues marked the stories of Plateau Indian students; and markers of elaborated discourse informed the stories of the white students.

Why these discursive differences would emerge so prominently in students' narratives of all kinds is partially answered in students' reports of their home lives, which reveal culture-distinct patterns of language socialization in early childhood. I argue that TV watching, rather than book reading, might effectively bridge the gap between home and school literacies, inasmuch as students at this multiracial middle school consistently drew on various narrative genres from the entertainment industry—the movie review and the video box blurb—and wove them into their own accounts of their lives. This case study also dramatizes yet another turn of the screw for the access issue: Although schools may be online, students at school too often are not. According to students' reports, their lives at home and at the community center are becoming immersed with electronic media. In fact, computer-mediated communication would be a more culturally consistent way of interacting and learning for Latino and American Indian students than the individualistic knowledge displays, such as speaking up in class, that typically dominate the traditional classroom—if only they really did have access at school, as federal reports indicate.

Can instructional technology realize its potential to transform student learning? That is the question under investigation in Chapter 5, "Revisiting the Access Issue." Updates in 2003 on the four schools featured in this book's case studies shed light on how the introduction of technology affected teaching and learning in these respective settings, not just in the short run, but over the long haul. Although the face and pace of change differed from school to school, these updates tell the same story: Change is only skin-deep without the technological resources and critical pedagogy to sustain it.

In sum, this book offers new insights into teaching writing and literature, at once academic and practical, based on institutional crossings of the digital divide. These crossings all involve connecting high-poverty schools with the Carnegie Foundation's Research 1 universities, either through a writing center or a teacher preparation program. The crossings analyzed in this book are primarily social and discursive, and only sometimes electronic. In effect, putting the two sides of the divide—the underserved and the overprivileged—in contact, if not always in dialogue, opens up a view from the other side of the digital divide, but this time from the perspective of the underserved. Because of the Internet, either directly or indirectly, the "have-nots" can speak for themselves, and in so doing, they can teach educators at all levels much about nonwhite ways of knowing and interacting in the world.

CHAPTER 1

Reconsidering the Terms of the Debate

Whoever controls the terms of the debate controls the debate.

I remember one of my professors making that statement in a graduate course on William Faulkner back in the late 1980s, for reasons I have long since forgotten. And I remember that statement every time I read or hear talk about the digital divide—which is to say, I have had occasion to remember it many times since the mid-1990s, when *the digital divide* first became synonymous with *the access issue*. The metaphor of a great chasm— a divide—polarizes the issue as a matter of simply having, or not having, access to the Internet. From there, it is easy to categorize whole groups of people as "haves" or "have-nots." Unfortunately, the public policy debate on access usually comes at the expense of the "have-nots," in large part because the terms of the debate thus far have been defined and controlled by the "haves."

But that need not be the case. The metaphor of a divide could also serve as a reminder that a vast gap does indeed separate rich and poor in this country, and that gap is at once economic, racial, discursive, and epistemological in character. Resituating the divide within the landscape of larger social and political formations should allow for a richer, more complicated discussion of a host of issues that attach themselves to Internet access per se but are actually constituted by these larger formations. By first retrieving the original rhetorical context for the digital divide and then examining how this construct in turn spun off yet more binaries in the public debate on access in the late 1990s and early 2000s, perhaps we can reinvigorate not just the terms of the debate but also the debate. We can do so only if we add in the other half of this conversation from the "have-nots." Adding this new perspective aims to restore some balance to the conversation, which is prerequisite to any systemic change. Reopening the terms of the debate should also open up new understandings of the impact of Internet access on public education, especially for those schools that serve communities distant from the mainstream, as I will explore in subsequent chapters.

CONSTRUCTING THE DIVIDE

The issue of access long preceded the metaphor of the digital divide. The lack of computer access was noted in the early 1980s when Tandy and Apple II computers first appeared in the schools. The Internet itself, however, was largely inaccessible to all but those in government and academic circles until the first graphical Web browser, Mosaic, was introduced in 1993 and made the World Wide Web a much easier place to visit (Compaine, 2001a). In 1995 the information "have-nots" began to capture national attention. That year, the first of four federal reports on computer and telephone access was issued by the National Telecommunications and Information Agency (NTIA). In 1996 the Clinton-Gore Technology Literacy Challenge called for every school in the nation to be wired by the year 2000 (Selfe, 1999). At about this same time, the term *digital divide* actually entered the public discourse. Its origin has been credited to Lloyd Morrisett, the former president of the Markle Foundation, although he himself doubts that he actually coined the phrase (Compaine, 2001b). The phrase turned up in print in 1996 as a headline for the *New York Times* article written by Steve Lohr. By 1998 it had become a metaphor for *the access issue*, appearing in the subtitle of the second of the four NTIA reports.[1]

Ever since the metaphor emerged, closing the digital divide has been an elusive national agenda, in large part because the definition of the divide itself is a "moving target" (Compaine, 2001b, p. xiii; see also Burbules & Callister, 2000). Access to what and from where has never been consensual or stable in the public policy debate. As the Clinton-Gore Technology Literacy Challenge soon discovered, simply counting schools connected to the Internet does not measure student access. Federal benchmarks soon shifted from counting connected schools to counting student-per-computer ratios and then counting computers per instructional rooms. Quality of access— 56K, T1 lines, broadband, and wireless—also became part of these measures. Simplistically constructed but variously defined and measured, the terms of the great debate on access and its most popular metaphor, the digital divide, thus became firmly entrenched in the public imagination in the latter half of the 1990s.

The series of federal reports by the National Telecommunications and Information Administration (NTIA) in 1995–2000 was largely responsible for this entrenchment. Created in 1978, the NTIA, which is part of the

U.S. Department of Commerce, was charged with conducting market research to shape public policy decisions in achieving the goal of universal telephone service capability; later its mandate focused on universal Internet service capability. To that end, NTIA contracted the Census Bureau in 1994 to conduct a survey of 48,000 households on computer ownership and online access, cross-tabulated for specific variables—income, race, age, educational attainment, region, and the three geographic identifiers, rural, urban, and central city. The first report came out in 1995, with the title *Falling Through the Net: A Survey of the "Have Nots" in Rural and Urban America*. Subsequent reports in 1998, 1999, and 2000 (with different subtitles) not only narrate the progress that has been made in achieving universal online service; they also speak to the national optimism about technology generally.

Taken together, the four reports implicitly tell a story of technological determinism: that technology is not so much revolutionary as it is evolutionary, and that evolution is inevitable, inevitably progressive, and progressively desirable (Feenberg, 1991; Selfe, 1999). National optimism in technology is both cause and effect of the *Falling Through the Net* reports. Collectively, the reports trace the progress that we as a nation have made toward achieving universal online services, verified through exhaustive statistical analysis, the statistics both speaking to and affirming our faith in rationalism and positivism, progress literally being made right before our very eyes. The implicit promise of "better living through technology" will be fulfilled when "everyone" has Internet access.

How *everyone* gets defined, described, and discussed in these reports reveals our continued struggle to reconcile the fact of systemic racism with the myth of merit, or more precisely our attempt (once again) to remedy systemic racism with individual initiative and hard work—the notion of bootstraps (Villanueva, 1993)—by supplying, in effect, the boots: not Internet access but Internet access "capability." The goal of a classless society where the digital divide is truly closed suffers the usual degradation in meaning from equality to equal opportunity to any opportunity at all, as analyses of these four NTIA reports will demonstrate.

The First NTIA Report: Profiling the "Have–Nots"

That the NTIA would expand the scope of its original mandate to include Internet service seems logical enough, given that connectivity in the telecommunications industry is dependent on the same infrastructure, be it wired (telephone or cable) or wireless. Less obvious perhaps at the time but more obvious now in hindsight is the economic agenda of the Clinton-Gore administration, which actively sought to reboot the economy of the early 1990s recession, seeing technology as a new growth industry, both domestically and globally (Selfe, 1999).

Still, it is hard to explain the language of the NTIA's first report in July 1995, entitled *Falling Through the Net: A Survey of the "Have Nots" in Rural and Urban America*. Its evangelical zeal goes beyond mere boosterism. In its opening paragraphs, the report strikes a tone of urgency, at first defensive for focusing almost exclusively on computer ownership and online services rather than on telephone service, as such reports used to, but quickly turning to a tone of advocacy with almost missionary zeal. The figurative language, too, seems oddly out of place in a government document otherwise mind-numbingly dense with percentages and bar charts:

> While a standard telephone line can be an individual's pathway to the riches of the Information Age, a personal computer and modem are rapidly becoming the keys to the vault. The robust growth recently experienced in Internet usage illustrates this promise as new and individual subscribers gravitate to on-line services. (NTIA, 1995)

The report goes on to elaborate on the profiles of all those gravitating "individuals," variously called "the have-nots" and "the information disadvantaged," always cited in quotes in this as well as in the subsequent reports as if to emphasize that these are "so-called" labels and not necessarily terms assigned by the document. Readers are encouraged to see these poor individuals as a group who tend to live in central cities and in rural areas.

> While most recognize that *poor* [emphasis in original] people as a group have difficulties in connecting to the NII [National Information Infrastructure], less well-known is the fact that the lowest telephone penetration exists in central cities. Concerning personal-computer penetration . . . however, no situation compares with the plight of the rural poor. (NTIA, 1995)

The "plight" of the rural poor, given the context, could mean that the rural poor have neither the infrastructure nor the cash for telephone service. Either way, the word *plight* seems melodramatic, given that telecommunication services are not absolute necessities of life, such as food and shelter, and even then plight would only appropriately describe lives of extreme want and despair. But having food and getting connected are often treated as equally important. According to UN Secretary General Kofi Anan, "People lack many things: jobs, shelter, food, health care and drinkable water. Today, being cut off from basic telecommunications services is a hardship almost as acute as these other deprivations, and may indeed reduce the chances of finding remedies to them" ("Bridging the Digital Divide," 1999).

The rhetorical turn to location—central cities versus rural—is a distinction underscored in the report's subtitle. In public discourse, those geographic identifiers in particular are usually code words for race: *central cities* = African American and *rural* = white. The common denominator for these locations is socioeconomic class. The implicit argument is that poor people, both poor whites in rural areas and poor blacks in the central cities, cannot afford access, period. This point effectively sidesteps the issue of race/ethnicity as a critical definer of the digital divide. The original report, however, cannot be blamed for constructing the divide simply along class lines, as is usually argued. In fact, the very next paragraph of the report does factor in race, layered on top of geography, but in very unexpected ways, never mentioning poor rural whites at all:

> An examination by race reveals that Native Americans (including American Indians, Aleuts, and Eskimos) in rural areas proportionately possess the fewest telephones, followed by rural Hispanics and rural Blacks (Table-Chart 4). Black households in central cities and particularly rural areas have the lowest percentages of PCs, with central city Hispanics also ranked low. (NTIA, 1995)

Cumulatively, the first report's summary on race and geographic location seems to ask readers to see the information in layers. Such a reading would suggest more than the simple fact that poor people do not have access; rather, it suggests that Native Americans, Latinos, and African Americans living in central cities and rural areas are disproportionately poor and therefore do not have access. In other words, race/ethnicity and poverty go hand in hand. But while the text invites readers to make the systemic connection between poverty and people of color, the next heading proclaims in boldface type, "The Facts," listing the "characteristics" of the "have-nots" as the following: Poor in Central Cities and Rural Areas; Rural and Central City Minorities; Young [Households] and Old; Less-Educated in Central Cities; and Northeast Central Cities and South. The problem with the report, here and throughout, is that these "characteristics" seem to describe separate groups of individuals. That problem can be attributed in part to the report's representation of information in bulleted lists as well as in numerous bar graphs, which isolate different variables. The text of its closing paragraph admits that this fragmentation is also attributable to the report's methodology:

> More work needs to be done to better assess the characteristics of these "have nots." For example, it is not clear whether the same low-income disadvan-

taged are also those who are minorities or the less educated or the young or old. Additional evidence is required for determining whether, e.g., mobility of households is an important determining factor of information exclusion within central cities or rural areas. (NTIA, 1995)

The last example—which asks to what degree "mobility" might account for exclusion—retreats from the larger suggestion of the previous sentence: that the characteristics of the "have-nots" listed and analyzed at every turn in the report in fact describe the same groups, all American minorities who are disproportionately poor and are excluded not only from the economic wealth of this country but also from the means for making wealth. In a closing paragraph subheaded "Empowering the Information Disadvantaged," the report returns to the bootstraps theme of the American Dream:

> NTIA's research reveals that many of the groups that are most disadvantaged in terms of absolute computer and modem penetration are the most enthusiastic users of on-line services that facilitate economic uplift and empowerment. Low-income, minority, young, and less educated computer households in rural areas and central cities appear to be likely to engage actively in searching classified ads for employment, taking educational classes, and accessing government reports, on-line via modem. (NTIA, 1995)

The direct correlation between being disadvantaged and being enthusiastic about online services is more rhetoric than reality (exactly the opposite is the case according to later reports, as will be discussed below) and more bootstraps than boosterism.

Subsequent NTIA Reports: Still Falling, Trailing, and Lagging Behind

The three subsequent NTIA reports are not as rhetorically and ideologically conflicted as this first one. The bootstraps theme continues, but seems more modulated and matter-of-fact; the benefits of the Internet are now an uncontested given of the conversation: "Information tools, such as the personal computer and the Internet, are increasingly critical to economic success and personal advancement" (NTIA, 1999). "These same groups also tend to engage in online activities that can result in their economic advancement, such as taking educational courses, engaging in school research, or conducting job searches" (NTIA, 1999). "Each year, being digitally connected becomes ever more critical to economic, educational, and social advancement" (NTIA, 2000).

Like the first report, subsequent reports continue to use the language of deficit, of lack, to describe the "have-nots," often in binary opposition to the "haves": "the information rich and the information poor"; "information haves and information have-nots"; and the "information disadvantaged." The second report (1998) describes "the least connected." All the reports have the same main title, *Falling Through the Net*, a title that was probably first settled on because of its play on the word *Internet*, figuratively conceived as a net.

But what kind of net, exactly? A safety net for trapeze artists? A fishing net? What kind of net would have holes big enough in it to allow certain people or fish or trapeze artists to fall through? How hapless would one have to be to fall through a net designed to keep one from falling? In the second report new implied metaphors emerge for the "have-nots." Blacks and Hispanics "now lag *even further behind* Whites" (emphasis in original) and "Single-parent, female households also lag significantly behind." All of the various categories of "have-nots," at one time or another in these reports, "trail." The implied metaphor is that of a footrace, which insidiously suggests that all runners started from the same starting blocks, the same starting point, and how they compete in the race is a matter of self-discipline and natural (read: biological) ability and talents: "The information 'haves' [continued to] outpace the 'have nots'" (NTIA, 1999). "However, a digital divide still remains. The report shows that not everyone is moving at the same speed, and identifies those groups that are progressing more slowly" (NTIA, 2000). "Blacks and Hispanics, while they still lag behind other groups, have shown impressive gains in Internet access" (NTIA, 2000).

The language of business persists too, as one might expect in reports from an agency of the U.S. Commerce Department, but given the context of racial-ethnic poverty, this kind of language resonates in other ways to a nonbusiness, public audience. Consider the phrases, "pockets of 'have nots' among the low-income, minorities, and the young" (NTIA, 1998) and "groups that are most disadvantaged in terms of absolute computer and modem penetration" (NTIA, 1995). This is the language of invasion, imperialistic and sexual, at the same time. Unlike the footrace metaphor, where ethnic minorities and female heads of household have agency enough to "lag behind," notice the lack of agency ascribed to penetration. Penetration just is. The fourth report states that "Blacks and Hispanics . . . continue to experience the lowest household Internet penetration rates" and "large gaps for Blacks and Hispanics remain when measured against the national average Internet penetration rate" (NTIA, 2000). Here also agency is not ascribed to Blacks and Hispanics, unlike earlier descriptions of their persistent lagging behind. Like penetration, large gaps just are.

To be fair, subsequent reports are more modulated in tone, largely stripped of the footrace metaphor (with the exception of single-parent, female-headed households who still "trail" and "lag behind" all other categories of "the least connected"). The three updates on the digital divide trace how this national conversation evolved through the 1990s. In the second report, entitled *Falling Through the Net: New Data on the Digital Divide*, released in 1998 and based on data collected in 1997, talk of "individuals" is gone and the "have-nots" are more accurately understood as certain "populations." The "Profiles of 'The Least Connected'" are more detailed, with categories more broadly constructed and more clearly defined in terms of race, class, and gender, pointing to the overlap in categories. Thus the Rural Poor are one of the four categories of the Least Connected, but the Rural and Central City Minorities are described in terms of ethnicity as well as population-density location. Young Households, who were merely contrasted with the Old (over 50) in the previous report, are described as "below 25," "rural, low-income," and "with children" in this report, as well as the households most likely to be "particularly burdened." The fourth category of Least Connected is Female-Headed Households, described only as single-parent and female, with those living in the central city the least connected of the single-parent, female-headed households when contrasted with dual-parents and single-parent, male-headed households. No mention is made of income levels of these various household configurations—the point of comparison (and the onus of inadequacy) being single females heading up households in central cities (translation: black single mothers on welfare).

The third report, entitled *Falling Through the Net: Defining the Digital Divide*, released in 1999 and based on 1998 data, is much more detailed both in its data and its analysis of that data. The subtitle might have been more appropriate for a first report; coming as it does with this third report, it reflects the growing attention to identifying exactly who the "have-nots" are. The issue of school access, first mentioned in the second report, gets much more attention in this one. And for the first time, a distinction is made and data is collected on owning a computer and having that computer connected to the Internet, with additional research on why certain categories of personal computer (PC) owners are not connected: The primary reason cited is "don't want," but exactly why certain owners "don't want" access is only tentatively examined. Also for the first time, this report collects data on usage: How are Americans using this access, and how is that usage tied to various identifiers?

The third report follows the bad news–good news rhetorical strategy of a political sermon, as it were, a one-two punch enjoining its national audience to pull together and keep working toward the ideal: universal access. In this move, socioeconomic class and affordability dominate the debate, and with the problem thus defined, the solution becomes quite simple: dropping prices on machines and on connectivity. After reporting the bad news that the digital divide has not gone away—and doing so with apparent chagrin—the report gives readers the good news lest they despair to the point of inaction, rallying them instead to renewed effort:

> Nevertheless, the news is not all bleak. For Americans with incomes of $75,000 and higher, the divide between Whites and Blacks has actually narrowed considerably in the last year. This finding suggests that the most affluent American families, irrespective of race, are connecting to the Net. If prices of computers and the Internet decline further, the divide between the information "haves" and "have nots" may continue to narrow. (NTIA, 1999)

The report's analysis of this collected data is insightful and productive not just for the business community but for educators as well, drawing important connections and beginning to flesh out a more robust understanding of access: different kinds of access (home, school, work) and different uses of that access (e.g., information retrieval and communications). Among those insights is that those using computers to communicate either personally or professionally are more likely to have home access than those using computers to retrieve information in public settings. The second report tended to conflate the different uses of the Internet (e.g., "Policymakers should continue to focus on connecting these populations so that they too can communicate by telephone or computer") but saw the poor using the Internet for information retrieval (e.g., "These populations are among those, for example, that could most use electronic services to find jobs, housing, or other services")—presumably, the kind of information that would enable the poor to float their own boats out of poverty.

The most neutrally worded report of the four reports is the fourth: *Falling Through the Net: Toward Digital Inclusion*, released in October 2000. The bootstraps theme from the earliest report, which holds the individual responsible for his or her own fate, emerges once or twice, but talk of "groups" dominates.

And for the first time, this report points to, and provides evidence for, a startling finding: that maybe the "have-nots" don't want access. It ends on that note, an ending that signals perhaps a new direction for talk about the digital divide, a beginning of a fresh conversation, where the terms of the debate are not entirely framed by the "haves." In many ways, the digital divide, at least as it has been framed throughout the 1990s, might be the ultimate digital distraction (Applebaum, 1999), displacing other conversations that might reconfigure the issues in more complex and illuminating ways.

RECONSTRUCTING THE DIVIDE

The *Falling Through the Net* reports, therefore, are more nuanced and in-conclusive than one might have thought. Their rhetoric and representation of information can be blamed to some degree for the rhetorical construc-tion of those pesky "have-nots," a construction that has persisted beyond the NTIA reports and into popular discourse on the divide. This public discussion at times in the late 1990s and early 2000s has verged on expand-ing the understanding of the access issue. But each of these expanded and contingent conversations, at first rich in complexity, has narrowed into oversimplifications that once again yield oversimplified answers. Thus the "divides" multiply in this ongoing debate—and always at the expense of the "have-nots"—in conservative returns to the same racist-classist as-sumptions. In retracing some of those arguments, we can perhaps also re-suscitate the conversation beyond those conclusions and beyond those as-sumptions, taking into account the view of the divide from the other side, the side of the "have-nots." Such a view will allow us not only to excavate the ethnocentricity on the access debate generally, but maybe—just maybe—to wrest control of the debate itself, with the ultimate purpose of shaping public policy, especially as that policy affects access in high-poverty schools as well as in the communities of color they serve.

Have-Nots Versus Don't-Wants

As early as 1999 (based on data collected in 1998) the NTIA reported that owning a computer and using the Internet were two different categories of usage: stand-alone computing (i.e., word processing, spreadsheets, games, CDs) and connecting to the Internet (i.e., accessing the Web for informa-tion, entertainment, and shopping). And the primary stated reason for not connecting to the Internet was simply "don't want," as pointed out above. Who were the "don't-wants"? The report that followed in 2000 briefly notes without elaboration that "even when adjusting for income, Blacks and Hispanics are less likely to have Internet access at home." The issue of whether or not everyone *wants* access represents an important new dimen-sion to the debate on the digital divide. Unfortunately, the "don't-wants" have fared even worse in this debate than the "have-nots," for there is just no excuse, apparently, for (wrong) values. You cannot save someone who does not want to be saved, the underlying assumption of this argument goes.

Why the "have-nots" with money would be "don't-wants" is most often understood as a lack of diverse content on the Web. Disregarding other digital technologies and other uses of the Web for just a moment, let us examine this point more carefully. James Porter and others have noted that the access issue needs to also take into account "community acceptance" (Porter, 1998, p. 103), meaning that cyberspace needs to be hospitable to newcomers, ready to embrace and socially accept the "technopoor" (Gravill, 1998). Business has responded to that call for hospitability, seeing the don't-want issue as simply a matter of content. For example, in 1997 the Black Entertainment Network and Microsoft partnered to provide content for the African American community, joining the well-established Net-Noir and American Visions for this niche market, also known as "narrowcasting" ("Sites Aim," 1997). As competition for audiences heated up, new audiences had to be sought out and courted with new angles. The strongest of these niche markets were gays and African American communities. Why? According to one entrepreneur, "'Those populations are always seeking voice. . . . For the ones who feel in some way they don't have full access these forums provide a way to congregate and discuss issues that the real world don't provide very easily. Quite frankly, I wasn't aware there were so many African Americans online. This is an easy way to come together, and it's empowering'" ("Sites Aim," 1997).

Voice and empowerment were not the only things these sites were selling, of course, but soon a plethora of sites tailored for these and other niche markets sprang up, "everything from churches and businesses to record labels" (Cochran, 2000). "If people don't feel that there is something there for them, then they have no reason to go," says 28-year-old Darien Dash (quoted in Cochran, 2000), who once promoted rap artists, but went on to run the first publicly held African American Internet company. When the news came out in 1998 that the divide was widening at lower income levels, the CEO of NetNoir was not worried: "This expectation of everyone having equal online access immediately today is almost juvenile," he said. "This industry is only three and a half years old. In 1998, I'm very comfortable with the fact that affluent black people have computers and non-affluent black people don't" (quoted in Nichols, 1998).

Such sites featured a host of services and unique technologies, catering to upscale tastes, not to the tastes of the poor. Voice and empowerment are clearly not being marketed to the poor, for whom a very different usage is advocated in the public debate on the digital divide. As one study conducted by the nonprofit Children's Partnership has pointed out, for the poor, the Web remains largely irrelevant for many good reasons: "lack of most urgently needed local information"; literacy barriers; language barriers; and cultural diversity barriers ("Online Content," 2000). These "content barriers" intersect in Catch-22 ways. For example, "most urgently needed local information" is not available on the Web, in part because there is a paucity of jobs in the local areas, and in part because keeping such information up-to-date would require costly Web maintenance and a dedicated staff position, and in part because such information simply is more easily and reliably obtained on the street and through the grapevine ("Online Content," 2000). Further, those with higher socioeconomic status have historically adopted communications technologies more quickly than those of lower socioeconomic status, when access was based on an open market. This "usage gap" becomes a self-stoking cycle; as more entertainment and advertisement spring up on the Web for Latinos, for example, more proficient groups are targeted for the latest in networking and problem-solving tools (Hacker, 2000). Cheap Internet appliances too are evidence of the "dumbing down" of technology for previously underserved customers. A case in point was Audrey, an Internet appliance small enough to sit on a kitchen countertop, presumably to make it (her?) more user-friendly for women; for example, Audrey "giggled" when the user made a mistake (Marriott, 2000).

The disinclination of the "don't-wants"—a group that includes both affluent and poor persons—to use the Internet has been explained in many ways besides lack of diverse content. Forrester Research reported that this population lacks "technological optimism" (Brady, 2000). This lack of optimism in computers should not be conflated with *technophobia*, a label often ascribed to racial minorities in a rhetorical move that suggests people of color are primitive. A number of studies have dispelled these old connections. For example, African Americans and Latinos spend more on premium channels of cable television than other demographic groups; and even though fewer African Americans are online, they spend comparable amounts per capita on Internet shopping (Marks, 2000). Others have described this disinclination for computer technologies as a "psychological barrier" that must be confronted. "The digital divide is no longer just about technology, it is also about psychology. It is about persuading people of all ages to take advantage of what is offered" (Cochran, 2000). Notice how this accounting for the "don't-wants" turns on the bootstraps assumption that essentially "blames the victim" for being poor.

A more compassionate but still paternalistic version of blaming the victim is *not* blaming the victim, who after all cannot help himself, the logic goes. Rather, the victim is so benighted as to not know what is good for himself and for his financial future, at least not without major coaxing. Some have gone so far as to suggest that economic and racist bases for the digital divide do not exist; the issue, they say, is "not a lack of access to technology but a lack of interest in technology. The educational system does not adequately address that lack of interest" (Steele-Carlin, 2000). From there, it is just a short and logical step to constructing a "values divide" where the "have-nots" do not have the right values, unable to see far enough in the future to make wise choices today. Even if they were given "boots," they would sell them on the streets for short-term cash: "You can give a person a computer, but if they do not see its value in their life and do not know how to operate it, chances are good that they will sell the computer to produce cash—something that everyone sees a personal value in" (Steele-Carlin, 2000).

Conversion Stories. Nonetheless, the late 1990s and early 2000s saw a rash of feature stories on the "have-nots"/"don't-wants" arriving at enlightenment and joining "everyone" who sees personal value in technology. These conversion narratives serve the ideological interests of the "haves" and the corporate elite, not those of the poor, upon whom it is incumbent to "change [their] Internet outlook." Take the example, typical of the genre, of Normajean Hickok, the self-described "Internet dummy." "[I] didn't want to learn because it was really scary." The story continues:

> But after earning only $13,000 last year, she took a chance on a computer-training course for low-income people. In exchange, she was given a computer and is already earning money at home working for a medical billing company. She believes she can make big money for herself and her 8-year-old son.
>
> "When I finish the training that I want to take," says Hickok, "I can see myself being able to get a job making $50,000 or $60,000 a year."
>
> Hickok has bridged the digital divide, but millions of Americans have not. Even in the high-tech heaven of California's Silicon Valley, companies cannot find enough computer-literate workers—and that shortage is costing them more than $3 billion a year.
>
> Poor neighborhoods were always a part of Silicon Valley but light years away from the high-tech companies. Those companies are now turning to these neighborhoods for workers. . . .
>
> Private industry has joined with the government in providing computer equipment and training to the poor. But the digital divide is no longer just about technology, it is also about psychology. It is about persuading people of all ages to take advantage of what is offered.
>
> President Clinton visited a center today called Plugged-In for a reason.
>
> After a slow start, Plugged-In now attracts regulars like Tanika Milligan, who goes online for everything from job postings to e-mail chats. And it is relatively inexpensive, at only a dollar per day to come in and use the computer facilities. "Yeah, it's worth it," says Milligan, smiling, "It's really worth it."
>
> But what about all those people who are still scared to cross the digital divide, as Hickok was?
>
> She offers this advice: "If you can read and you can type, you can do what you need to do on the computer."
>
> Hickok adds that if she can do it, anyone can. (Cochran, 2000).

"The reality is if you're not plugged into the Internet in the near future," says Ruben Barrales, the president of Joint Venture in Silicon Valley Network, in the same article, "you're going to be unplugged from job opportunities, unplugged from consumer opportunities, from finance opportunities" (Cochran, 2000). Only one of those claims—more consumer opportunities—is a reasonable outcome from a computer literacy course. What are the real chances that Hickok will make $50,000–60,000 in annual income after this course or even a couple of such courses? Although that scenario is unlikely, if it did happen, that opportunity would more likely come on a subcontract, temporary basis, perhaps as a homebound telecommuter, an employment model that is being favored in a volatile e-economy looking to cut labor costs by not providing health care and retirement benefits.

A flurry of these conversion narratives whirled just before and after the dot.com bust of March 2000, suggesting that this kind of hard-sell strategy was part of and consistent with the search for new domestic markets, rather than the global market, as originally envisioned by the Clinton-Gore economic revitalization plan of the 1990s. Technological globalization proved more problematic as a business model. Besides infrastructure limitations, the "have-nots" of the world were much too poor for American and multinational corporations to expect a return on the capital outlay for wiring vast areas of jungles, tundra, mountains, and farmland. Domestically, however, that strategy could work because of government subsidies and public policy mandating universal school access.

Technological Faith. How can we reinvigorate the debate on why some groups do not want to use the Web—even when the Web has more diverse content, even when people are computer literate? We need a better understanding of why so many have so little "technological optimism." How do people come to have that kind of faith in technology and become active users of the Internet?

In thick descriptions of how individuals become computer literate enough to want Internet access, several principles emerge. First, computer literacy requires a certain confidence that is gained only by spending time online; thus those with experience get more experienced, and those who do not have that opportunity do not achieve the threshold facility necessary for computing—a reinforcing cycle of exclusion and inclusion (Burbules & Callister, 2000). Second, social circumstances dictate who has that time, or has power to allocate time, in their schedules to work and play online. Often these circumstances systematically exclude certain groups. Those working in a networked office or university are more likely to experience access in a manner qualitatively different from those working on farms or in factories or raising children at home (Burbules & Callister, 2000). Even if they have an Internet-connected computer sitting in a corner of the barn or break room or den, they do not have the same support available to those working in offices or those participating in online communities.

On one Listserv of scholars and teachers interested in technology and rhetoric, one discussant told the story of two different couples living in a working-class trailer park. The couple in graduate school spent about 20 percent of their annual income on computers one semester; while the other couple, who worked in a factory, spent about 20 percent of their income on jet skis. Neither could understand the other's priorities. The factory-working couple obviously did not see the value of computers, either for leisure or for work, because computing had absolutely nothing to do with the way they made their living. Nor were computers worth their entertainment value, at least not compared to water sports for the family. What looks like a real division in values in this case is in fact a real division in livelihood where many newcomers first have "access" to leisure, work time, and opportunity.

According to Cynthia Selfe and Gail Hawisher, who have collected narratives from members of marginalized groups, some individuals within those groups may be late in joining the computer revolution for a variety of reasons. Often, some combination of race, poverty, gender, and location factors make a difference in the lives of these individuals (e.g., women of color who live in poverty and in rural settings). The stories of such individuals indicate that they often had their first access from public use in higher education classrooms and open labs. From there and with that education, some of these individuals acquired jobs that required computer literacy skills; they then may or may not have purchased computers for home. All of the individuals that Selfe and Hawisher interviewed indicated that personal motivation and family literacy values also affected their digital literacy values and practices (Selfe & Hawisher, personal communication, September 27, 2002).

Other studies confirm the nexus of education and work access for novices. One study at Vanderbilt University that focused on factors influencing computer ownership at home confirmed the later government finding that after controlling for income and education, whites are more likely to own computers than African Americans. But significantly, the study also found that "education explains access to a work computer" and that "African Americans in the upper income brackets—more educated, younger, and more likely to be working in computer-related occupations . . . are more likely than whites to have computer access at work after taking income into account" (Novak & Hoffman, 1998). Thus, at higher income and education levels, whites have more home access than African Americans, and African Americans have more work access than whites.

But I want to suggest another way to think about these racial variables in home and work access found in the Vanderbilt study. It would seem that, for African Americans, having work access is enough. Or, put another way, African Americans, *even* those with work access (the usual way people come to want and buy computers for home use and acquire "felt need" for the Internet) may resist "computer penetration" at home as a matter of cultural bias. This bias goes beyond a simple matter of irrelevance, to which the industry has already responded with more ethnocentric content sites. Rather, I argue throughout this book that the values divide is actually a culture divide in complex ways. Domestic time and space are used differently in large families and in communities where family interaction is maintained daily, as the analysis in Chapter 4 will demonstrate. Further, the etiquette and desirability of sharing information online (and off-line) are culture specific; thus the allure of the Information Age where information circulates freely is lost on many African Americans, a point I will return to in depth in Chapter 2. And finally, although the computer industry is dominated by a white corporate elite and the Internet has been described as "fundamentally alien" to women and people of color ("Digital Divide," 2000), the "have-nots" nonetheless import their own ways with words and interaction patterns to online environments in school settings, as Chapter 3 will explore.

Race Versus Class

Among the most prevalent of the divides this larger debate has spawned is the race versus class binary. Of course, this binary has dogged poststructuralist academics as well as the popular press on any number of issues. And it is a rhetorical construction that seems to give the Left more trouble than the Right. To talk about race as a determining factor for anything—from expressive culture to economics—is to run the risk of perpetrating racist stereotypes. African Americans are not a monolithic community. Nor are Latinos, and even naming such a large group as a single entity dismisses important differences in national identities, histories, and cultures of Central and South America. Conversely, privileging socioeconomic status whitewashes the critical differential of race. Many, in fact, would argue that the very term *race* should be dropped altogether because the term has no basis in biology; in fact, there is more physical and cultural variation *within* a racial category than *between* racial categories (Fox, 2001). But using the term *ethnicity* is too broadly misconstrued to include Euro-

Americans, whose skin color does not mark their difference on sight and whose histories and cultural values closely align with those of the American white majority.

Race, as I use the word in this book, refers to people of color, specifically African Americans, Latinos, and American Indians, all of whom as groups have been historically excluded from the matrix of power and wealth in this country. They are indeed the "least connected" electronically, socially, economically, politically, and historically. Asian Americans also suffer discrimination, especially for one or two generations, as have other immigrant groups historically before becoming assimilated. The label *model minority* ascribed to Asian Americans discounts their struggle to survive and thrive even as it is used against African Americans, Latinos, and American Indians who are accused of not trying hard enough. But lumping Asian Americans with these other minorities also discounts the latter's status as "involuntary minorities" and the bloody history of these groups in the United States. As Victor Villanueva (1993) explains, "structural assimilation" (p. 24) depends on three factors: (a) the history behind a minority group's entry; (b) the number and distribution of those attempting to assimilate; and (c) their physical and cultural characteristics. Minorities, as opposed to immigrants, have experienced slavery, conquest, and colonization. That "history of subservience" (p. 31), coupled with distinctive racial and cultural attributes, mark African Americans, Asian Americans, Latinos, and American Indians for discrimination and caste-like status, even if individuals within the first three of those groups have voluntarily immigrated to the United States.

In the *Falling Through the Net* reports, the statistical and graphical breakdowns for race and income (as well as education, age, and so on) have exacerbated this particular divide in public thinking, blinding readers to the overlap in the two categories. "It's not a question of race, it's a question of income," said Jeff Chester, executive director at the Center for Media Education. "While there are significant numbers of people at the poverty level who are minorities, it's not their minority status that contributes most to their lack of access to technology; it's their economic status" (quoted in Nichols, 1998). Seeing the problem as a matter of income makes the solution simple: dropping prices. Lavonne Luquis, president of Latino Link, believes "the problem will take care of itself in time. As prices continue to drop, Internet presence will be ubiquitous in households five years or so out" (quoted in Nichols, 1998). Further, African American leaders have protested that depicting the technological gap as "a black thing" fuels the stereotype of the hopeless, helpless black victim in need of government rescue. One leader has pointed out how the statistics are automatically read as a white-black narrative, although the "facts" could yield another story:

"Instead of showing a predictable black-white gap, technology research reveals that Asian-Americans, not whites, have the highest Internet and computer use. And while blacks at most income levels lag behind whites and Asians, it's Latinos, not blacks, who are the least likely to be wired. But no one's worrying aloud about an Asian-Latino digital divide" (Hubbard, 2000). Another commentator accused President Clinton for playing the race card when he announced during his State of the Union Address in 2000 a new federal program called ClickStart to insure lower computer and connectivity charges to the poor: "[Clinton is] hoping to inflame minorities so they'll go to the polls next fall and support Democrats" (Berst, 2000).

The George W. Bush administration's chair of the Federal Communication Commission (FCC), Michael Powell (son of Colin Powell), apparently did not have the same agenda as that of the Clinton-Gore administration. When asked his policy and position on the federal programs to close the digital divide, Powell called the phrase "a dangerous term." "I think there is a 'Mercedes divide,'" he said. "'I'd like to have one; I can't afford one.' I'm not meaning to be completely flip about this. I think it's an important social issue. But it shouldn't be used to justify the notion of essentially the socialization of the deployment of the infrastructure" (quoted in Chuck 45, 2001). Setting aside the issues of (a) whether or not Mike Powell could afford a Mercedes if he wanted one and (b) why he chose that particular brand of car to construct his own metaphorical divide, consider more closely his remark: The Mercedes would suggest that the divide is a matter of money; at the same time, it calls up racist images of welfare queens driving Cadillacs to pick up their government checks, a narrative that is nonetheless race-coded without ever having to mention race.

The larger point of Powell's first press conference, where he made the Mercedes remark, was that the new FCC under his guidance would be more hands-off than the FCC of the Clinton-Gore administration. But "socialization of the infrastructure" at this point in the history of the Internet would actually mean *de*privatization and *re*instituting public regulation of a project originally created and funded by the federal government in the first place. Just as the transcontinental railroad systems of the nineteenth century were funded by public money and then sold to private industry, public policy under the Bush administration threatens to continue welfare as we know it: corporate welfare, that is. The rhetorical divide of race versus class persists, then, in this now-you-see-'em/now-you-don't way that proffers the advantage of deniability: I'm not talking about race; I'm talking about class, so I can't be accused of racism.

Nonetheless, the digital divide almost always gets visually pictured in terms of race, even when the accompanying story never mentions color, focusing instead on socioeconomic status. Take, for example, the cover of

Wired's December 12, 1999, issue, which featured a bewinged and nude black female diving off a cliff. Arresting as the cover image is, the accompanying story is just a one-page article on the business model of free access at portal sites in exchange for personal information and persistent advertising. The cover story's title "Net Free for All" is a clever play on words, not only capturing the free access angle of the story but also suggesting riotous conditions concomitant with looting. The closing paragraph reads, "Still, some wonder how long the free ride can last, especially with the growing glut of free-but-at-a-cost computer and Internet access offers. Even in the Net economy, there's no such thing as a free launch" (Ratliff, 1999). That last phrase, of course, puns on "a free lunch," which like "free ride," suggests a something-for-nothing mentality—a common mind-set of the e-generation perhaps, but one that is explicitly connected, by way of the image on the cover story, with people of color. Ironically, as one letter to the editor mentioned in a subsequent issue, the wings on the female figure are not broad enough to keep her aloft; she is doomed to fall just as the business model of free access was bound to fail.[2]

Penetrating Pockets. While the NTIA reports focus on "penetration" and on "pockets of 'have-nots,'" it is not too much of a leap to think that "penetrating the pockets of have-nots" is the subliminal message here. The "digital divide" has achieved the status of a marketing slogan to three different audiences at once, telegraphically selling social justice to the public and bootstraps to the poor. The third audience is the private business sector, who needs to see evidence that the hard sell to the public and poor is creating demand, that the demand will be there if they supply the infrastructure. In short, if they build it, will they come? And if they do come, will the revenue be enough to offset the tremendous cost of getting infrastructure in rural areas in particular?

When the *Falling Through the Net* reports, as well as the popular press, talk of economic advancement, one must ask whose economic advancement is really at stake. Corporate interest in the digital divide is obviously motivated by the need to develop new markets, especially as computer penetration hit saturation points in the early 2000s (Compaine, 2001a). Sometimes press releases and news reports connect the campaign to close the divide to market forces; the ones who need to be assured that the "have-nots" represent a viable new market is venture capital and the private sector, perhaps even more so than the public and the poor. "There's a huge undeveloped market out there," said a technology center manager for the New York Housing Authority (quoted in Marks, 2000).

The interdependent chicken-egg relationship in this government-sponsored ad campaign to close the divide is clear in the following excerpt, where the news of the closing gap butts up against the news of rising confidence among venture capitalists:

> Computer and Internet use among African-Americans and Hispanics is increasing at a rate so stunning the gap could be closed in a few short years. That's spawning a host of investments in Web sites aimed at minority communities. And confidence is high among some venture capitalists and experts that as market forces move in to exploit those untapped communities, the overall technology gap will close even faster. (Marks, 2000)

In the following news report, one can see how the market forces in the digital divide work in concert: bootstraps for the American Indians and tax breaks for Internet service providers (ISPs). What is not apparent is where the money ultimately winds up.

> The Comprehensive Rural Telecommunications Act will likely be taken up by Congress next session. The act is intended to help spread the economic benefits of the digital age to Indian reservations and small cities—those with populations of less than 20,000. . . . ISPs that agree to provide broadband Internet access to the centers would receive a tax break equal to 10 percent of their expenditures on the facilities. Enhanced providers—those that transmit voice and data of up to 10 Mbps—would be eligible for tax breaks equal to 15 percent of expenditures. The act should open up new markets for broadband providers, who have found that the markets in big cities have become flooded. A similar effort, the FCC Indian Initiative, would give ISPs tax incentives for bringing broadband services to Indian reservations. ("Small-Town Broadband Allure," 2000)

In a news release announcing a program to provide access to the Navajo in Shiprock, New Mexico, for just $1 a month, the comment that American Indians are disproportionately poor is casually juxtaposed with the mention that "meanwhile" Microsoft is "donating" software to bridge this divide:

> Poor American Indian households already qualify for a discount, but Clinton administration officials said the cost is still too high for many. Nearly one-third of all Indians live in poverty, compared with 13 percent of the U.S. population.
>   Meanwhile, Microsoft Corp. announced Sunday it is donating more than $2.7 million in software and cash to help bridge the "digital divide" and economic disparity between Indian tribes and wealthier segments of society. (Gearan, 2000)

Shiprock, New Mexico, was President Clinton's second stop on one of his last official tours, which was tellingly called the New Markets tour. The tour took him first to East Palo Alto, where the computer ratio in 2000 in the schools was 1:28 and 24 percent of the children lived in poverty—a place not geographically far but racially and economically light-years away from Palo Alto, the heart of Silicon Valley. The symbolism was of course the reason for choosing this site for kicking off ClickStart, a partnership of federal government, community centers, and the computer industry (Gearan, 2000). What is not mentioned in this news report are the details of ClickStart. The ultimate goal of the ClickStart partnership was to provide online home access to the 9 million families who receive food stamps. The U.S. Commerce Department would issue monthly vouchers of $10 to families on food stamps, with children, and without a computer. The family would match $5 a month and receive a scaled-down computer and Internet access for 3 years.

Following the Money. If we follow the money, we see that the companies "donating" the computers will receive the $15 ($10 from the government; $5 from the family) a month, which comes to $540 after the 3 years—about what computers would probably cost in 3 years' time. Notice, too, to whom the money is *not* going: the community groups responsible for the tough, ongoing training and technical support piece of the program (Oppenheimer, 2000). Thus the money is not going back into the community at all, but back into Silicon Valley and its back channels. The rich get richer; the poor get poorer; and the real divide widens, not narrows. "We all know there are people and places that have not fully participated in this new economy. I see these places as places of opportunity," Clinton said. "If we can create new employees, new businesses, new jobs, new opportunities, we can keep the American economy going" (Gearan, 2000). The point, after all, seems to be keeping the new economy going, not redistributing the wealth generated by the new economy.

If we are indeed intent on closing the digital divide systemically, we need to find ways to insure that federal dollars go back into the community. As reservations and inner-city community centers come online, as food-stamp recipients get home access, federal dollars need to stay in those communities, with contracts awarded to minority-owned businesses within those communities. Mescalero Apache Telecom provides a good example of this model. "The tribalization of telecommunications goes way beyond dealing blackjack to tourists from Texas," says Godfrey Enjady, the general manager of the company, which plans on ringing the reservation with fiber-optic lines for high-speed connection. This infrastructure, Enjady explains, will "attract investment in the same way an emerging market needs to lure

foreign capital" (quoted in Romero, 2000, A1). At least half a dozen trib-
ally owned telecom companies now serve their own reservations, with aid
from special federal subsidies. Unfortunately, such companies are not ex-
empt from outside competition; any company that serves tribal lands can
also qualify for federal aid (Romero, 2000).

Home Versus School Access

ClickStart marks a radically different tack in public policy on the digital
divide, focusing as it does on home access rather than on school access. In
1996, the Clinton-Gore administration announced the Technology Literacy
Challenge, calling for all the nation's schools to be wired by the year 2000
in an initiative called Kickstart (inspired by the program name Head Start).
The issue of home versus public access is first mentioned in the second
Falling Through the Net report, with the acknowledgment that efforts to
provide universal access, the express mission of the NTIA in the first report, will have to concentrate on providing public access, not private: "Because it may take time before these groups become connected at home, it
is still essential that schools, libraries, and other community access centers
. . . provide computer access in order to connect significant portions of our
population" (NTIA, 1998). The felicitous understatement that "it may take
time before these groups become connected at home" implies that access is
simply a matter of time—time to get in the infrastructure.

While it may seem logical, even humane, to focus on schools that serve
the "have-nots" in the meantime, such attention does not necessarily work
toward dismantling the basis for the divide in the first place: a racist-
classist society where wealth, not just income, is unevenly distributed. To
believe that access will ameliorate the lot of the poor is to believe in the
myth of literacy, with its bootstraps logic: that is, getting a good education
will mean getting a good job, which in turn will lead to upward mobility
(Gee, 1990; Graff, 1979, 2001; Selfe, 1999; Street, 1995). The key word
in that equation is *good*. Getting a good education in a high-poverty school
is oxymoronic for all kinds of reasons, as have been rehearsed most dramatically by Jonathon Kozol (1991).

Computers and connectivity in the schools too often are being used
to reproduce the usual capitalist relation between management and labor
(Aronowitz & Giroux, 1993). Having digital resources has not necessarily
changed classroom practices on either side of the divide, or at points in
between: White, wealthy, suburban schools tend to use computers for communication and collaborative learning projects—learning experiences that
will prepare them to take professional and managerial roles in their working futures—while poorer schools tend to focus on keyboarding and dril-

ling on CD-ROMs—learning experiences that will train them to take orders (either at fast food keyboards or from their future managers, schooled
probably in the suburbs) (Cuban, 1986, 1993, 2001; Ohmann, 1985; M.
Warschauer, 1999). And of course, no matter how much equipment is fun-
neled into poor schools, those students will still be at a disadvantage compared to students from richer schools, who have home access. Middle-class
students already come to school with linguistic and learning competencies
that favor school success; having home access just adds to those strengths.

Wiring and equipping high-poverty schools does serve agendas other
than closing the divide. Besides preparing future workers, computers in the
schools are also preparing future consumers. As Lester Faigley has suggested (in the context of Microsoft's donations to schools here and
abroad), that corporate plan is not unlike that of the Jesuit missionary
movement: "Give me a child of seven and I will give you a Microsoft user
for life" (quoted in Faigley, 1999, p. 129). Further, the children are bringing pressure to bear at home, as shown in this narrative of a father who is
looking to improve his lot by taking a computer literacy course via an
interactive program sold by IBM:

> A maintenance supervisor at a church in Harlem, [Gregory Davis] says that
> just four months ago his 12-year-old daughter knew more about computers
> than he did. Today, after taking an intensive computer-literacy and repair
> course, Davis is confident that each click of a key is bringing him closer to a
> future that was once unimaginable: becoming a network engineer. "I see what
> I want to do now, and I'm working incessantly to reach that goal," he says.
> "A network engineer can start at $90,000 a year." (Marks, 2000)

School children and their families are more time-distant markets under development, compared to the here-and-now multibillion dollar education
market, which is selling computers and applications to schools, who in turn
are cutting back other programs to make room in their budgets (Moran &
Selfe, 1999). Such a payout could be worth the investment, if these new
resources are used in transformative ways. Stories such as the one cited
above, however, should make us pause to ask what kind of education and
what kind of jobs will school access ultimately provide. If we cannot answer "better" for both questions, then efforts to close the divide by way of
the schools will be misguided as well as misleading.

HEARING THE OTHER SIDE

We could also ask better questions about how to use computer technologies to effect systemic change. At bedrock level, the access issue is merely

symptomatic of the real divide in this country, that is, the maldistribution of wealth. All claims to the contrary, the New Economy of the 1990s actually exacerbated, not narrowed, that chasm; and after the dot-com bust of 2000, the maldistribution of wealth has stabilized at historically high levels (Holmes, 2000).

In fact, the connection between educational attainment and income has always been problematic. Education and stratification research has long sought to explain the complex relationship between socioeconomic factors (such as parents' education, income, and aspirations for their children), race, and children's education outcomes. A consistent finding is that Asian Americans and Euro-Americans achieve higher levels of education than other ethnic groups, even when controlling for income and parents' educational level (Entwisle, Alexander, & Olson, 1997). Such a "racial gap" plays easily to cultural (i.e., "the values divide"), racist, and biological explanations, such as *The Bell Curve* (Herrnstein & Murray, 1994).

The most recent research, however, has identified inherited wealth—not income—as a more direct determinant of parents' aspirations and strategies for their children's education. While income may allow families to live in better neighborhoods and thereby afford their children access to better schools (Kozol, 1991), inherited wealth insulates families from the negative impact of job loss, illness, and other unexpected expenses, which can easily derail family plans for education and retirement. Parents in one study have said that if they had assets, their primary goal would be to expand their children's educational opportunities (Oliver & Shapiro, 1995). Conley (1999) found that African Americans are more likely than whites to be expelled from school and less likely to finish college, but when controlling for wealth (not just income) and parents' education, that racial difference in educational outcomes disappeared.

A likely explanation for the inequities in wealth is this: white couples inherited wealth, while nonwhite couples did not (Hooks & Blair-Loy, 2000). Generational poverty due to systemic racism insures that certain groups never accumulate enough wealth to pass on to the next generation. Thus unequal distribution of wealth through multiple generations could explain racial differences in educational attainment. If that hypothesis proves correct, "then educational reforms that do not directly address this maldistribution . . . will likely continue to confront a perplexing and troubling 'racial gap' in educational aspirations and outcomes, *even among children in households with similar incomes*" (Hooks & Blair-Loy, 2000; emphasis in original).[3]

Insofar as we are hard-selling the economic benefits of Internet access to the poor and the public as "the key to the vault," to recall the words of the first *Falling Through the Net* report (NTIA, 1995), we are selling false goods. Instead of selling the economic benefits of connectivity, we should speak more pointedly—and could do so in much better faith—about the educational benefits of *inter*connectivity between students, between classes, between schools, and between schools and universities. Such connections crisscross the digital divide, bringing the underprivileged and the overprivileged in contact, not just as individuals, but as groups, communities, and institutions. To be sure, making these connections is no easy task, given both the disconnect between educational institutions and also the very real consequences of the lack of access of all sorts—to the Internet, to human resources, to time, to money, to power. When all these conditions do conspire to make interconnectivity possible, the insights gained need to be shared with the profession and with the public.

The chapters that follow aim to do just that. They offer qualitative case studies of four high-poverty schools as they enter the Information Age and interact with outsiders, variously defined. These case studies feature a tiny portion of a mountain of student writing that I have amassed from institutional crossings of the digital divide for several years. The student writing in many ways speaks for itself, but it also raises the hard question that dogs us as English educators: Given the systemic conditions that support a racist world, how then do we actually teach writing and literature? The pedagogical implications drawn from student writing, online and off, is what this book is really about.

The online projects that I analyze in the chapters that follow provide a critical perspective from the other—nonwhite—side of that question so important in English education today. For the divide is not just racial and economic in character, but also social and discursive. As high-poverty schools come online, they write in ways consistent with their own rhetorical traditions, traditions largely intact because of the relative linguistic isolation of impoverished communities of color. My hope is that this fresh critical perspective will inform classroom practices in ways that enable all students to think more critically and creatively about their words and the intersections of their worlds with others. Pedagogy is political, whether we want to face that fact or not.

Of course, neither connectivity nor interconnectivity nor research studies thereof will rectify the systemic inequities undergirding the divide. That correction will not happen in our lifetimes, or even in the lifetimes of our students. Nor are the educational benefits of connectivity really economic, as the hype on the digital divide would have us believe. But that fact does not absolve us from acting now to transform literacy education as we have known it. Computer literacy is certainly a job requirement for most indoor work, but learning the tool is not the same as being liberated by the tool (Victor Villanueva, personal communication, June 26, 2003). And liberation, or what Paulo Freire called critical consciousness, should be our ultimate goal in the classroom. As English educators, we need to stay focused not on literacy but on critical literacy. After all, in just 30 hours of instruction, Freire was able to teach illiterate Brazilian peasants to read and write *and* become politically awakened (Brown, 1987). Surely over the course of a student's secondary school career, we can too.

CHAPTER 2

Putting One's Business on Front Street

Technology always bears the values of those who produce it. The gun or the Great Wall of China presupposes a certain kind of resolution of conflict, just as a medieval cathedral presupposes a certain understanding of spirituality (Feenburg, 1991; Porter, 1998). The same principle holds true for digital technologies. Hardware and software metaphorically reconstitute the world of their designers, often rendering a reality inclusive of their experience but exclusive of the experience of the technological underclass (Selfe & Selfe, 1994). The graphic interface of the Windows and Macintosh operation systems—with its desktop and file folders—maps out a white corporate world alien to many people of color living in poverty, among other groups (Selfe & Selfe, 1994). In like manner, referring to a computer's pointing device as a mouse may be an especially loathsome association for new users living in impoverished central cities plagued by rodents.

But design is not destiny. Although designers build new technologies in the images of their own worlds, new users from other cultural groups nonetheless bring with them their own customary ways of knowing as they approach and acquire new media. A classic example is the "hole-in-the-wall" experiment in India. A computer was put in a wall facing a garbage-strewn lot where poor children played. The children quickly learned without any guidance how to use the computer, inventing their own terminology for the icons. They called the mouse pointer *sui*, the Hindi word for "needle," and the hourglass icon a *damru*, the Hindi word for "Shiva's drum" (Judge, 2000). A *New Yorker* cartoon (May 28, 2001, p. 85) illustrates this same principle of user-centered perspective. Two dogs are studying a computer screen on an office desk. One dog is seated with its paw on the mouse; the other, standing beside the seated one, says, "Let's see if we can't scatter the trash all over his desktop." Thus views of the other side of the digital divide can expose the ethnocentricity of much of digital culture generally, including the metaphors that animate it.

31

Besides hardware and software, emergent literacy sites also offer opportunities for new user-centered perspectives, especially as underrepresented groups come online. Of these emergent sites, electronic mail (e-mail) may prove to be the most important for literacy development as well as for literacy studies. The medium enables communication across discursive communities, and when these discursive communities exist in asymmetrical relations of power, the communicative space of e-mail creates linguistic contact zones. These zones can also become sites of resistance for the less powerful. In these new spaces, the less powerful can selectively appropriate, merge, or infiltrate the idiom of the more powerful. The texts they produce "often constitute a marginalized group's point of entry into the dominant circuits of print culture" (Pratt, 1991, p. 35). Rather than focus on what literate conventions will emerge in the space of e-mail, however, we might also ask whose literate practices will prevail, merge, or fade away.

This chapter takes a critical look at one cybermentoring project between writing tutors at the University of Michigan (UM) and tenth-graders at Detroit High School (a pseudonym) in the mid-1990s, when the implicit rules governing appropriate linguistic behavior in person-to-person e-mail were still very much up for grabs. To properly contextualize the electronic record that came out of this project, a theoretical framework that appreciates the perspective of the technological underclass is needed. Working within this framework, one can gain fresh insights into the racial parameters bounding information sharing in personal e-mail. These insights hold important implications for writing teachers and tutors, whether or not they are working in African American–majority classrooms.

THEORETICAL FRAMEWORK

E-mail is often described as a cross between speech and writing, with features of both recombined and extended to produce a new discursive field altogether (e.g., Aycock & Buchignani, 1995). But for the study at hand, I prefer to think of e-mail simply as conversation. Such a frame is a reminder that e-mail is an interaction between two or more people, drawing at least some of the attention away from the formal, static features of the text itself. In other words, thinking of e-mail as conversation can shift the focus from the *forms* and onto the *norms* for appropriate linguistic behaviors in this new literacy site (Sloane, 1999). This starting point also strongly suggests that e-mail texts might be most productively analyzed using a sociolinguistic approach.

For sociolinguists, the unit of analysis is the speech community, not the formal features of language itself; its goal, to identify and describe "cultural patterning of communicative conduct" (Hymes, 1974, viii). This approach provides a way for seeing how norms deeply inform the forms, which after all do not constitute absolute standards so much as they reconstitute the asymmetrical social structure upon which those standards rest. Thus sociolinguistics, with additional perspectives from cultural anthropology and social psychology, can provide an interdisciplinary heuristic for exploring the real gulf enacted in electronic contact zones. That gulf is not just between formal and informal writing conventions or even between oral and written literacies but between discursive communities (Eldred & Fortune, 1992).

Further, thinking of e-mail as conversation will also make the discussion in this chapter more culturally relevant than thinking of e-mail as a written genre. The study at hand examines a specific feature of African American culture: the etiquette of information sharing in oral settings and how that etiquette gets imported into electronic spaces for audiences at different distances. When individuals approach new media, they bring with them their past attitudes and habits of minds, often folding in old practices to form new ones (Sloan, 1999; Haas, 1999). When a discursive community is introduced to new media, individual histories vis-à-vis technological innovation become less important than the community's expressive culture and political history as well as that community's historical access and attitudes toward technological innovation. Insofar as e-mail is seen as conversation, that conceptualization might better explain what kinds of literate behaviors many African American teenagers will bring to bear to this new discursive space.

LOCAL CONTEXTS

The UM/Detroit project connected 27 tenth-graders in one English class at Detroit High School with 27 writing tutors who were junior and senior undergraduates at the University of Michigan in 1996–97. As a codirector of the tutoring program and the UM/Detroit project, I not only trained and supervised tutors but also made site visits to Detroit High School on a regular basis during 1994–1997. During those site visits, I worked with administrators, technicians, teachers, and students. Thus I was in a unique position to both observe and participate at many levels over a sustained period of time.

The goals, sponsorship, history, and major players of the UM/Detroit project are largely irrelevant to the study at hand, so I need not go into those details here.[1] Nevertheless, certain features of the project's design proved crucial to constructing a linguistic contact zone where race-based differences in interpersonal communication are still visible and can be examined in the electronic and paper archives of the project. These archives, as well as my own observations and notes taken at the time, serve as the primary material for my qualitative analysis in this chapter.

All of the Detroit students and their teacher were African American; 25 of the UM tutors were white, 2 were African American/white, and the 2 UM supervising faculty (my colleague George Cooper and I) were white. Although the one-to-one e-mail exchanges continued for a little more than one calendar year, the portion of the project under study in this chapter is a 5-month period, December 1996–April 1997. The two groups of students also met in person, first in Detroit in February 1997, and then in Ann Arbor in April 1997. During that period, the UM tutors worked with Detroit students as they prepared their portfolios for American College Testing (ACT). ACT was piloting its new portfolio system, and Detroit High School was one of its pilot sites.

The UM tutors offered individualized writing instruction, using the principles of Online Writing Lab (OWL) pedagogy developed during the UM-OWL's early history.[2] But unlike an OWL, where clients and tutors are randomly paired for each online conference, the UM/Detroit project partnered Detroit students with UM writing tutors for the duration of the academic year. By keeping the dyadic pairings together, we thought, the human connection might more closely approximate a mentoring relationship rather than simply a tutoring one. In fact, the project was often referred to as *cybermentoring*, which was a novel term at the time that captured sponsors' attention, imagination, and ultimately substantial financial support.

Several factors, however, disrupted the continuity that the project sought to insure. First there were the differences in institutional calendars. Besides different start and end dates, the two institutions also had different spring and winter breaks, and additional time was taken out at the high school for state testing, snow days, professional development days, and so forth. In addition, absenteeism limited online time together, especially in the winter months, when Detroit students could not get transportation to school on city buses so full that buses do not stop at designated points (public and school transportation are combined in Detroit) and when Detroit students are especially prone to illness because of malnutrition, poor housing conditions, and inadequate health care. Other factors also exacerbated absenteeism rates, such as after-school jobs and family child care responsibilities.

But most of the lost time online was caused by technical difficulties at the high school. These difficulties included inadequate electrical wiring (the entire wing that housed the new computer lab was eventually rewired) that prevented having all the computers running at the same time; printers that could not be networked; district-centralized server problems; and inadequate on-site technical support (personnel who also happened to be hostile to the project specifically and low-income African Americans generally). A larger issue was the problem of providing e-mail capability in a school district in the days before the advent of Web-based e-mail. With over 250,000 students in the district, the central instructional technology (IT) team was understandably reluctant to set up individual accounts on centralized servers.

Ultimately, Locke Carter from the Daedalus Group (one of the project's sponsors) came up with an ingenious work-around solution: launching Eudora from individually assigned diskettes, which could be passed out when the Detroit students came into the computer classroom and taken up when they left. All the students' e-mail was stored on these diskettes, unless they deleted messages, either on purpose or by accident. An unintended consequence of this work-around solution was that students' diskettes became an accidental archive (albeit a partial one) of the project. Students' diskettes were unexpectedly released to me after the project's end in May 1997.

Besides "hard-side" technical issues, such as downed servers and power failures, the "soft-side" issues of working with a techno-poor population posed another layer of difficulty. Many of the students had never touched a computer before, much less used e-mail, and doing e-mail launched from a diskette requires a relatively high level of computing skills. Locked diskettes, damaged diskettes, deleted critical launch files, and misread or mistyped e-mail addresses—all of these common problems disrupted the flow of the e-mail conversation between the two institutions.

Given these circumstances, it is a wonder that any e-mail was exchanged at all. But it was, and in greater numbers than is usual for other OWL-like projects that I have since been involved with. Online projects between universities and schools are notorious for nonparticipation for at least a couple of good reasons. First, students have limited access to computers at school, and therefore online interinstitutional projects quickly lose momentum. In the increased lag times between exchanges, the immediacy of e-mail is lost, and the exchanges never achieve the back-and-forth feel of a conversation. Second, shyness and intimidation impede the potentially personal touch of e-mail, both among students, who are disinclined to "talk" to college tutors, and among teachers in public schools, who often find the exchanges intrusive or even threatening to their authority and expertise. Thus the institutional context usually mediates the medium to a debilitating degree.

These conditions held true with the UM/Detroit project, but in context-specific ways. The Detroit students had daily access, but that access was unreliable, for reasons noted above. And the shyness that is a typical hindrance in cross-institutional online projects might be more appropriately described as xenophobia in the context of Detroit, a city under siege by bad press and burned by hard economics for 30 years after the 1967 riots.

To give a sense of how hard these economics were in the mid-1990s, I will digress briefly to describe the city, neighborhood, and school context of the project. In the words of one journalist, Detroit is "America's first major Third World city" (quoted in Sugrue, 1996, p. 270). As the poorest urban area in the world's wealthiest country, Detroit lost almost half of its population between 1950 and 1990 (Henrickson, 1991). In 1995, about a third of its residents lived in poverty (Sugrue, 1996). Still, over 100,000 people—two-thirds of whom are African American—call this downtown area home, with an average family income of $9,870 (Toy, 1994). At the time of the UM/Detroit project, almost half of the population in the school's neighborhood was living at or below federal poverty level, more than half did not have high school diplomas, and a third were unemployed (Sugrue, 1996). Detroit High School itself reflected similar economic demographics. With a total student population of over 1,800 at the time of the UM/Detroit project, 63 percent were living in poverty, and approximately 10 percent were unofficially homeless. Two out of three students did not have telephones in their homes.[3]

One other demographic fact proved important to the project's outcomes. Detroit High School is a citywide school, a designation meaning that any student in the district might choose to attend. And many of them did, according to the principal, when word got out that the school had two computer labs, making it not only the first wired school but also the most wired school in the district at the time. This fact is important because students in the UM/Detroit project came from a broad socioeconomic range, including the high-rise projects in the immediate neighborhood as well as less economically depressed parts of the city.

Given these distinct obstacles and this distinct school and community context, participation rates in the UM/Detroit project were better than one might have expected. The electronic record from which I will be taking purposeful sampling in this chapter includes 215 messages in all, including 42 "papers"—that is, responses to assignments, from journal entries to formal essays, and revisions of this written work, re-sent for additional commentary from the UM tutors. This "paper" work was copied and pasted into e-mail messages, sometimes with accompanying remarks, usually about the assignment. More than half of the 215 messages came from the UM tutors, and the word count of their messages far exceeded that of their Detroit counterparts, who sometimes responded with just a single line. Further, these 215 messages constituted the e-mail between only 18 of the 27 pairs, two-thirds of the students involved. The other third include Detroit students who could not participate because of inoperative diskettes, lack of computer skills, lack of writing ability, or, most notably, resistance, as I will explore at the end of the chapter. And that third also includes UM tutors who did not participate in a timely fashion because they felt overwhelmed either by the task at hand or by academic and personal pressures of their own.

Besides the electronic record, the students' paper portfolios also became part of the primary material for this chapter. The teachers allowed me to photocopy several students' portfolios in progress that would ultimately be sent to ACT portfolio scorers in Iowa City at the end of that year. Some of the portfolios were written by students not in the online project. Although the portfolios were incomplete when I photocopied them, they still yielded 45 papers. Interestingly, none of these papers were sent to the UM tutors for online conferencing, or at least not on any of the diskettes that survived, a point I will return to later in the chapter. This paper collection adds yet another level to my analysis, especially when this work is compared to what was sent to the UM tutors.

It is true that the electronic archive does not represent all the interactions between students. It is impossible to know even approximately how many messages in all were deleted, purposefully or not. And not all diskettes were released to me for copying; some were lost or broken or thrown away. However incomplete, this accidental archive is large enough and representative enough to show us much about the implicit decorum of information sharing governing the linguistic behaviors between these two groups of students, interacting in an asymmetrical power relation in an institutional setting.

A key feature of the project's design—the online, one-on-one conference—was both its boon and bane. The personalized conference format aimed to personalize instruction, but in so doing, it also implicitly privatized it. Or at least that was the default assumption of the UM tutors. From the outset, their insistence that this communication was private made it difficult for us (George Cooper and me), as the UM tutors' supervising faculty, to direct their work. The view from the Detroit students, however, was exactly the opposite. From the outset, they treated e-mail communication as they did all communication, oral or written—to wit, as acts of public, personal information sharing. Exactly why the two groups, students and tutors, would make such different assumptions is the issue to which I now turn.

THE DECORUM OF INFORMATION SHARING

What kind of personal information can be appropriately shared and solicited between two or more people? When conversants are working from divergent cultural frames, the situation is ripe for cross-cultural miscommunication, but especially when those frames are constructed along white and African American race lines, where group identifications, historically defined by oppression and in opposition, tend to take over personal subjectivities.

According to Thomas Kochman (1981), the etiquette governing interpersonal communication is racially marked.[4] When strangers meet for the first time at social gatherings, a white person might make conversation by asking direct questions that attempt to locate a new acquaintance within a social, professional, and educational network that possibly intersects with her or his own. Inquiring about someone's livelihood, residence, marital status, family, and education are common questions considered appropriately sociable. But to many African Americans, such questions reveal whites' preoccupation with social status, which mistakenly assumes that material success derives from one's exertions alone. Talk of social status suggests that the speaker takes credit for her own success, without regard for the people, the blind luck, and God who got her there. If the speaker is African American, it might be said that such a person has forgotten where she came from or that she is "acting white."

Instead of questions inquiring of one's social status, as is commonly done when whites meet strangers, in African American culture, a person gets to know another by indirectly sizing up that person's abilities and attributes. That information may be in evidence through a person's actions, in words or deeds. Or a person may offer that information, in effect, bragging on his accomplishments, but he can do so without approbation only if those accomplishments are obvious or can be readily verified. His personal achievements are implicitly attributable and credited to God who endowed him with natural talents and abilities and to the home community who guided his growth. Personal success is community success, measured not so much in the material possessions of one person as in spiritual achievement of the whole community. But in white culture this kind of self-assertion violates norms of modesty and self-effacement and might be disparagingly referred to as bragging or showing off.[5] In sum, disclosing information about one's abilities and attributes in African American culture is considered appropriate if such claims can be backed up, but sharing information about one's social status and possessions is considered uncouth and arrogant; on the other hand, in white mainstream culture, the two kinds of personal divulgences carry exactly opposite value.

Possibilities for cross-culture miscommunication extend beyond the occasion of first meetings and casual encounters, however. With longer term acquaintances, many whites will typically inquire about what is going on in friends' lives, whereas many African Americans strictly guard that kind of information. In African American culture, to disclose one's current circumstances is disparagingly referred to as "putting one's business on Front Street." According to Roger Abrahams (1976), the word *business* has been a loaded term in African American culture at least as far back as antebellum America. Then as now, business has to do with "name" maintenance. One's business is considered proprietary; therefore, only the person who owns the information can initiate disclosure. For someone else to solicit it from another person, especially when the interlocutor suspects that such information may be embarrassing, is said to be "fronting" that person—that is, putting him up for public ridicule. Thus direct questioning about another person's business, especially about another person's station in life or current events or relationships in that person's life, is viewed as rude, intrusive, threatening, or even hostile.

Other unspoken rules define topical appropriateness in white and African American conversation.[6] Even though in the "'survey culture' of white America" (Abrahams quoting Grimshaw, 1976, p. 7), direct questions can be asked about almost anything, certain topics are not broached in polite company in white mainstream culture. For example, one might inquire about another's family but not about another's sex life or income or, in certain social strata, a woman's age. In contrast, many African Americans might be comfortable talking about their sex lives, incomes, and hourly wage, but not about their relationships with their parents; and they might be more willing to talk about whom they know but not what they do for a living (Abrahams, 1976). Even when the topic is culturally appropriate, the conversational routine of direct questioning suggests certain power relations for many African Americans, among other cultural groups. Among peers where a degree of reciprocity and equal status has been established, asking a direct question might be taken as an invitation to engage in a playful exchange wherein certain information might be embedded and therefore appropriately shared in a way that can be enjoyed by all (Abrahams, 1976).

The only proper way in African American culture for someone else to coerce another to share his business on Front Street is by *signifying*. More than just asking indirectly or just hinting, as might be done in white mainstream culture, signifying also connotes a degree of verbal inventiveness, irony, or humor. Although signifying indirectly solicits information, it also provides a face-saving mechanism for both parties involved: The interlocutor can appear to be "just joking," in which case both parties might laugh and shrug off direct confrontation. If a person does not want to answer, she may respond with silence, perhaps walking away without emotion (to indicate, essentially, "You're not talking to me" or "Your question does not touch me; I'm cool") as a way of rebuffing the interlocutor. The other option is to lie, a response that takes spontaneous inventiveness. "Lying" more closely equates to story-telling or what Heath (1990) calls "quasi-fictional narrative" (p. 501). Rather than being viewed as untruthful, lies are valued as entertainment that showcases a person's verbal agility. In white expressive culture, this kind of lying is akin to making a sarcastic retort or telling a tall tale. The cultural difference is that in white main-stream culture, this kind of witty comeback might be misjudged as a challenge that exacerbates tensions; whereas in African American culture, it would more likely defuse the tension of the moment (B. Monroe, 1994).

This culture-specific disinclination to offer or ask for information is a distinctive language socialization pattern in many African American homes and communities. Parents do not engage in question-and-answer routines with their children, as do many middle-class white parents. Instead, according to Shirley Brice Heath (1990), children are expected to listen rather than talk, learning "to judge when and to whom to give information and to be 'wise' and cautious about answering 'foolish' questions" (p. 501). Parents rarely ask children what they did or what they were doing, unless they do not know that information and want or need that information. As Heath explains, "The display of knowledge through talking about what was done could invite ridicule or punishment, unless offered as a poetic, clever, entertaining, and quasi-fictional narrative that could be jointly constructed by initiator and audience" (p. 501).

Sharing Personal Information in Class

The UM/Detroit project immediately ran up against these cross-cultural differences governing personal disclosure, even before the tutors and students got online together. On the first day in the new computer classroom, the teacher at Detroit High School assigned a variation of the widely used "biopoem" activity as an icebreaker to start off the school year with her own students.[7] Instead of writing the biopoems about themselves, however, students were told to turn to the persons sitting next to them, ask the questions, compose the poems about their neighbors, and then post those poems over Daedalus Interchange, a synchronous chat program. At that point, presumably the class would ask additional questions or simply offer words of welcome to newcomers to the class community. Here is the biopoem format the students were supposed to use in surveying their neighbors:

Line 1. First name
Line 2. Four traits that describe the person
Line 3. Relative ("brother," "sister," "daughter," and so forth) of
_____
Line 4. Lover of _____ (list three things or people)
Line 5. Who feels _____ (list three items)
Line 6. Who needs _____ (three items)
Line 7. Who fears _____ (three items)
Line 8. Who gives _____ (three items)
Line 9. Who would like to see _____ (three items)
Line 10. Who lives _____ (where)
Line 11. Last name

The first class flatly refused to do the assignment and protested vigorously. Several said specifically they would not put their business on Front Street, nor would they get into anyone else's business, no way. The issue was still unresolved when the bell rang to change classes. For the next class, the teacher tried introducing the lesson differently. She carefully explained that she was not asking them to put their business out there, nor was she asking them to get into anyone else's business. Even so, many in the second class voiced their objections. At that point, the teacher rescinded the questions altogether and told the class to introduce the persons sitting next to them in whatever way they saw fit. And they did. But their introductions revealed nothing particular or personal about each other's current affairs. In one instance, a student introduced her neighbor by way of telling her favorite color and her favorite movie, but she made no mention of her neighbor's obvious advanced stage of pregnancy.

Sharing Personal Narratives Online

The personal narrative assignment—the first major writing assignment of the semester—met with similar difficulties. Although some students did produce their papers, "they just told stories," the teacher explained to me, shaking her head in good-humored exasperation, meaning they told quasi-fictional narratives or "lies" unrelated to their lived experiences. Further, only a few ventured to send their narratives via e-mail to their UM tutors, who did not know exactly how to respond without the appearance of prying. For example, a Detroit student wrote about visiting her father, who was divorced from her mother and who had remarried. As she sketchily explained in her paper, after the divorce, her father apparently became very successful financially and moved to an exclusive suburban neighborhood. The writer bitterly faulted him for forgetting where he came from and for abandoning his community in the process of moving up and moving out. Her UM tutor, however, misread this narrative of "selling out," seeing it instead as a rags-to-riches success story. Accordingly, the tutor asked for more details to flesh out the paper, with questions about the father's livelihood and background training that prepared him for success—exactly the wrong questions to ask.

These were just a few of the most obvious and literal examples of students working from different cultural frameworks governing information sharing in the UM/Detroit project. Cross-cultural and interpersonal miscommunication played out in more complicated and nuanced ways in the e-mail conversations and in the assigned writings the Detroit students shared online. As I will show, race-based differences in conversational decorum hold validity across socioeconomic class lines in African American Detroiters' culture; likewise, it seems to hold across public and private venues and for both written and spoken communication. No matter what the venue or form, any communication has the potential for public dissemination. This public potential is inherently threatening because it portends that personal information can be passed on and disseminated on Front Street, where one's image is always at stake. Disclosing certain information in the right context allows a person to manage his own self-presentation, but doing so in the wrong context threatens to compromise that personal control.

But certain variables, inadequately explained in previous scholarship, also have bearing on the etiquette of information sharing. One such variable is the respective genders of the conversants and the degree of affiliation between them. Females working with females in the project, even if they were just newfound friends, seemed to have greater cultural permissions to share personal business—in fact, disclosure may be used to validate growing affiliation—whereas male students working with female tutors were the most guarded of all. More importantly, proximal distance, insider-outsider status relative to African American vernacular culture, and social domain also shaped the interactions between tutors and students; taken together, these factors account for the near total absence of the use of African American English (AAE) in the electronic record, despite the fact that all the Detroit students were native speakers of AAE. These findings hold important pedagogical and curricular implications for tutors and teachers working with African American students, in class or online. I will discuss that topic at the end of this chapter.

THE E-MAIL CONVERSATIONS

As discussed earlier, the UM/Detroit project was organized around dyads, one student from each institution assigned to work together for the course of a school year. The e-mail conversations within those dyads, however, cannot be solely understood as interpersonal communication, for they also represent intergroup communication, first and foremost, even in dyadic interaction, with individual psychology playing only a supporting role.

Interpersonal Versus Intergroup Interaction

According to social psychologists, examination of dyadic interaction should look to the group as the unit of analysis, rather than the individual, especially in situations where perceptions play a causal role in the behavior between individuals. Those individuals must feel affiliation to a special social category or feel they are perceived to be members of that special category. Such perceptions may give rise to stereotyping and ultimately prejudice, but they are nonetheless a rational outcome of social conflict and intergroup competition, an outcome that derives from a strong sense of group membership (Turner & Giles, 1981). Group identity is forged by "sociostructural" (p. 15) forces—that is, historical, cultural, political, and economic pressures, which ultimately shape consensual beliefs of an in-group relative to its out-groups: "real intergroup relations presuppose *shared* social categorizations and stereotypes, with a specific *sociocultural* content, related to members' *collective purposes* and the explanation, justification and evaluation of *concrete political and historical contexts*" (p. 27; emphasis in original). In this model of intergroup contact and conflict, stereotypes are not so much biases as they are heuristics, representing "the reservoir of cultural wisdom upon which the individual naturally draws" to organize the world (p. 21). At the same time, these heuristics also maintain the distinctive values and honor the distinctive history of in-groups.

Interaction between members of different groups has both interpersonal and intergroup dimensions, of course, but almost no interaction is strictly personal in intergroup contact. When group-identification markers, such as nationality, gender, race, or even occupation, are more salient than individualizing distinctions, then interactants will be more likely to act from their group-identity positions. What would be the relative salience of interpersonal and intergroup identifications over interpersonal but faceless e-mail? The UM/Detroit project suggests that interactants work most consistently from their group identities, defined by both race and gender. Only in a few cases did this intergroup frame give way at all, in part perhaps because those few pairs were able to create personalizing personae and in part because of face-to-face contact when students from the two institutions met, first in Detroit midway in the school year and then in Ann Arbor at the end of the school year. The electronic record of the e-mail conversations dramatizes this online interaction as primarily intergroup, rather than interpersonal, and as such, it provides a solid ethnographic example of race-based differences in the decorum governing information exchange.

Private Versus Public Communication

In like manner, the tutors were not equally wealthy. Nonetheless, the socio-economic difference between the two groups of individuals remained vast. Aware of Kochman's (1981) formulation on the race-marked differences in getting to know someone (his chapter on "Information as Property" was required reading in my tutoring class), the UM tutors worked hard to play down the difference in socioeconomic status (SES) between them and the Detroit students. UM tutors very consciously avoided references to wealth or indications of wealth, but they sometimes failed to realize the economic implications of the information they were innocently conveying. Thus one UM tutor mentioned her love of the four seasons, especially winter, because her family always went skiing in the northern part of the state. The sport itself and its associated expense (let alone her reference to the resort up north) is one that inner city youth would find foreign to their experience and impossible on their sustenance budgets. Another UM tutor spent Christmas in Cancún but tried to downplay that fact by explaining how she missed the ritual of being with her family in a cold clime for that holiday. Another talked about how excited she was to get a Discman for Christmas, something she had always wanted but could ill afford herself; but later in the same message, she announced her big news that her father's job was transferring him to France and that she and her brother were going to visit him and do a "whirlwind tour of Europe" before she had to get back to start her summer job.

These unconscious cues of wealth as well as the range of life experiences and circumstances did not escape the Detroit students' notice. In fact, very little escaped their notice, as they examined their messages from UM many times over, especially the first ones when the UM tutors introduced themselves. When the Detroit students opened these messages of introduction, they did not just read their messages aloud to their classmates and the many teachers and administrators and district IT personnel who had gathered to witness the first e-mail ever received at a school in Detroit; they *performed* their readings, often in falsetto voices and with much body English. These performances were classic examples of the speech event *marking*—making fun of a person by overdramatizing his speech and gestures (Green, 2002); the high-pitched voice, in particular, pokes fun at "authoritative discourse" (Hudson, 2001, p. 266).

The Detroit students seemed especially bemused by the UM tutors' unusual names and ethnic backgrounds, which some of the tutors chose to share with their students in these ice-breaking first messages. But the one bit of information that brought the house down was from one UM tutor who told her assigned Detroit student that she played the tuba and that she belonged to a group called the "tuba chicks." When that news was broadcast to the class by the message's addressee, those closest to him fell out of their chairs in turn, domino-like, each one mock-falling with different dramatic emphasis all the way down the row. And so on. The mood that first day of e-mail was celebratory rather than rancorous, and most of these spontaneous, public performance readings were done and received in much uproarious, good-natured fun.

In sharp contrast, the UM tutors read all of their messages from the Detroit students in private and alone. One reason, of course, was that the UM tutors had many points of access, including their own rooms, while the Detroit students could only access their e-mail in the computer lab at their school during class time. Further, although the UM tutors had opportunity to share their messages with their classmates as part of our class activities, most insisted on treating these messages as private because they were personally addressed, even though they knew that their own messages to Detroit were being treated as public communication. They seemed to accept that discrepancy with grace and generosity, and for good reason: The UM tutors were used to having their OWL conferences public to other OWL staffers and for peer-tutor training seminars. When I reported back to them about how their first messages were received, and how public that reception was, they seemed proud that their messages were attracting so much attention. As one UM tutor said, "At least our messages are being read." But most insisted on keeping messages from Detroit private, maintaining that they wanted to establish personal relationships with the Detroit students and felt that privacy was a prerequisite of building those relationships.

Female Conversants

Significantly, the most successful partnerships in this project were the female tutor–female student relationships, whether we measure success quantitatively (i.e., the number of e-mail exchanges) or qualitatively. In most of these introductory messages, the UM tutors tried to employ a rhetorical strategy that coupled information on personal attributes with information on social and family circumstances, as we see in the case of Chris and Ashley (both pseudonyms), cited below. In her first message to Ashley, Chris talks about her own feelings of excitement and uncertainty about the project in the first paragraph before providing some of the circumstances of her life in the end of the second paragraph, which nonetheless opens with her particular attributes and attitudes toward her major and her future plans. In pointing out details of her circumstances, Chris does so with subtle humor and with casual syntax ("I live in a house with six women [and my cat], I go to school and I have a part-time job waiting tables)."[8]

> Hi Ashley. I have just chosen your name from a hat (literally). My name is Chris Livingston and I am going to be helping you out with your portfolio (my official title is "cybermentor"). I've been looking forward to this "meeting" all semester—I've never done anything like this before and I'm excited to see what kind of work we can do together.
>
> I'm not sure if you know anything about me or why I'm doing this. I'm a junior at the University of Michigan and I'll be twenty years old this Friday!! I study English literature and I love reading novels and poetry. I also love writing. Everyone assumes I'm going to be a teacher after I graduate from college but I don't know about any of that yet. Right now, I live in a house with six women (and my cat), I go to school and I have a part-time job waiting tables. I grew up in Toledo, Ohio and I drive there often to see my family.

In mentioning the part-time job, Chris aims to undermine the wealthy UM stereotype that her assigned Detroit student may have assumed. Chris goes further to level the implicit hierarchy of the tutor-student relationship in her next paragraph, where she calls attention to the reciprocal benefit of the project:

> About this program—I am taking a class on peer tutoring and this is part of that class for me. So, while (hopefully) I'm helping you a lot with your writing, remember you are helping me too. I look forward to knowing you. Please reply soon!!! Tell me about yourself and ask me any questions you'd like.
> Hope to hear from you soon,
> Chris
> By the way, I just remembered that Chris can be a boy's or a girl's name
> . . . I'm a girl!

Chris manages to strike just the right note, slightly self-deprecating without being patronizing.

Ashley responds in kind, offering the same blend of circumstantial and attitudinal information, clearly collaborating with Chris to stake out common ground necessary for a budding affiliation:

> Hi Chris. I'm so happy that I get to finally to talk to you and write
> to you. This is going to be a fun experience for the both of us. When
> you told me that you had never done this before I had never done
> this before neither this is my first time to. Since you told me about
> yourself let me tell you about me. Well my name is Ashley Boudreau,
> I'm in the 10th grade my school I attened is Detroit High School. I'm
> 15 years old I'll be 16 years old on May 20th. I will be so very
> happy. I was born in Cincinatti, Ohio, I moved to Detroit when I
> was 2. My hobbies are going to the mall, watching t.v., talking on
> the the phone, listening to the radio, and hanging out with my
> friends. I think my life is pretty good. Do you like to do the other
> things that like me? Before I close up I do get good grades in school
> my G.P.A. is in 3.0's. That's what I forgot to mentioned.
> Hope to hear from you again soon.
> Ashley

Ashley's closing question actively seeks to continue the conversation. Although offering information about her good grades might be viewed as self-aggrandizing, her claims could clearly be backed up. Further, her mention of making good grades matches Chris's mention of having a part-time job with the same sort of studied casualness and probably for the same purpose, to disrupt stereotypic assumptions that everyone, consciously or unconsciously, brought to the project: that all white people are rich and do nothing all day, and that all black people are poor and do nothing all day.

A few of the female tutor–female student partnerships blossomed into strong affiliations, if not long-term friendships. At least one pair traded stories of family members with cancer, compared birthdays of family members, talked about upcoming weddings. One Detroit student's comment sums up best the rapport that only a very few managed to achieve over the course of the project. In her message she alludes to the day after the first face-to-face meeting—what she calls the "ceremony"—of the UM tutors and Detroit students at the high school in February:

> Before I get started I really enjoyed talking to you. I admitt I was
> strange in the beginning, but you kind or made me feel comfortable.
> I just received news that we don't have to do any work today. They
> feel very proud of us, I feel proud of myself. People who were at the
> ceremony told that it was aa great speech, it took a lot of courage,
> then again you know because you wer there. So I'll write to you on
> Monday (lunes). Hasta Luego Stephanie [a pseudonym].

Growing affiliation did not preclude cross-cultural miscommunication, however. In other female dyads, the Detroit students casually divulged personal information on their love lives and requested that kind of information from their UM tutors in the spirit of mutual confidences. The twin topics of boys and sex were frequently broached in these female-to-female conversations, both online and face-to-face (when the students met in February), as well as in some of Detroit students' assigned writings—so frequently, in fact, that some of the UM tutors became uncomfortable and ultimately offended. Although they came to me as a group to talk about their discomfort, they would not divulge details, in part because they were embarrassed by the information but in larger part, I think, because the information seemed to confirm stereotypes of African American women and the UM tutors did not want to appear racist.

But according to Tannen (1990), the sharing of intimate confidences is characteristic of women's talk, not just African American women's talk. Women often nurture budding relationships by, in effect, telling secrets. Personal disclosure in female conversations is not only evidence of friendship; it helps create friendship when the listener responds in kind. In their meager attempts to respond in kind, the UM tutors variously mention that they think "Brad Pitt is hot," "Denzel is cute," and "Antonio Banderas is fine!!!," but these fall under the "who-is-your-favorite-movie-star" kind of information. Clearly, the UM tutors could not meet the same standard of intimate disclosure set by the Detroit students. That discrepancy suggests that race and gender, not just gender, defined what topics may be properly broached in conversation with new acquaintances and in a school setting. At least for the young UM women, those two conditions constrained the conversation topic of sexual intimacy. They may have also felt constrained because of their positions as role models. Although offense was taken by the UM tutors, none was intentionally given, I maintain.

Issues of topical appropriateness—both "boy trouble" and material possessions—were combined with particular force in one instance, as can be seen in this next message. The Detroit student who sent the message openly disavows her cultural group membership, declaring quite emphatically that she is tired of this "GHETTO SHIT." Her putative Christmas bounty is fabricated (her teacher informed me) probably for the benefit of the UM tutor, with whom she aims to identify, rather than with the "low life scumbags" who live in her neighborhood. Here is her message:

Dear Megan [a pseudonym].
I had a great christmas also. I got a new T.V. a new coat, a coach purse, some perfume, some money, and a new VCR. And I had a

very happy new year. And now I'm in the second semester, and I
have more classes, and my work is getting a lot harder. My last report card wasn't so hot because I was under a lot of presure. I got a
2.7 which was really bad for me. Usually I usually get a 3.1 or better. I'm trying to stay in the 3.0 range, no 2.0's. Well anyway I've
made a lot of changes in what I do. My associates, my friends, and
my relationships. I had so many associates that just ment me no
good. And I have very few true friends. There are few people that I
can trust. And relationships, I'm finished with relationships for a
long time.

And were I live all I really see is low life scumbags that are just
loosers. The boys' and the men in my neighborhood are total loosers.
All they want to do is use the girls, and the women. To just have sex
with them, and talk about them. I have to constantly be on my toes
all the time. But I've changed that problem that I had with the loosers. I wasnt a different person. And what I mean by different a different race, and a person that has a better outlook on life instead of
hanging around in the hood getting into trouble. I'm not ashames of
my own but "I CAN'T STAND THIS GHETTO SHIT!"

In contrast, all the other dyads were mixed gender and shared little
or no personal information, very much guarding against fronting anyone.
Because females far outnumbered males in both groups, those same-sex
dyads predominated. Of the 27 pairs in the project, 18 were female tutor–
female student; 6 were female tutor–male student; and 3 were male tutor–
female student. In hindsight, I can see that at least some of the male tutors
should have been paired with male students; instead, names were simply
drawn from a hat. Although the male tutor–female student partners developed the most professional relationships and were among the most productive, the female tutor–male student partners were the very least productive.
The Detroit male students by and large declined to participate or participated by signifying. The different levels and kinds of participation are
forms of resistance but also forms of name maintenance, as I will show in
an examination of the assigned writings sent to the UM tutors.

THE ASSIGNED WRITINGS

Besides the e-mail conversations, the Detroit students' writing assignments
sent to the UM tutors electronically offers additional insights into cross-
cultural, interpersonal and intergroup communication. The implicit rules

governing personal disclosure in African American culture favor the person who owns the information, I want to reiterate, primarily to grant that person the power to construct and manage his self-presentation on Front Street. Information about a person might be divulged in more ways than one, for a person says much about himself by the way he "handles some grammar," in Zora Neale Hurston's phrase in *Mules and Men* (1935). In Hurston's sense, "handling some grammar" refers to a wide range of linguistic competencies, not just grammatical ones. These competencies might include verbal adroitness with *speech events*, such as "playing the dozens" (a verbal duel where two people familiar with each other trade insults that use the noun phrase "yo mama" or "your mother") (Morgan, 1998; Green, 2002); the mastery of certain *stylistic registers*, such as "fancy talk" and "trash talk"; and the ability to code-switch spontaneously between Standard American English (SAE) and African American English (AAE). The two varieties of English, of course, are mutually intelligible, but they differ grammatically, phonologically, and lexically. I will use the term *style-shifting* to refer to the adroit use of speech events and stylistic registers, which may or may not include switching between SAE and AAE, while I will use the term *code-switching* specifically to indicate shifts between SAE and AAE.[9]

A person's expertise in style-shifting is especially valued in African American culture. Competence entails not only *how* to switch styles; it also involves knowing *when* to switch styles and being able to do so spontaneously. Of course, all speakers in all kinds of speech communities employ a wide range of speech effects, both linguistic and paralinguistic, to show respect, mock seriousness, humor, role distance, and so forth. Such "fashions of speaking" (Hymes quoting Whorf, 1974, p. 175) are means of self-fashioning, and in African American expressive culture, this principle of linguistic self-fashioning is especially valued. Put another way, one's rap helps define one's rep on Front Street. Further, stylistic features hold social meanings in that the rules regulating their performance are highly sensitive to audience, social domain, and proximal distance. With the advent of electronic communication, that distance is at once geographic, social, and historical. In the work that the Detroit students sent to the UM tutors, we see many traces of the African American rhetorical tradition, most notably in the form of signifying and the homiletic stylistic register practiced in the black church; at the same time, we see only a few instances of AAE with any of its distinctive phonological, lexical, and grammatical features. The sociolinguistic dynamics of handling some grammar, in all senses of Hurston's phrase, hold important pedagogical and curricular implications for tutors and teachers working with African American students in class or online, as I will explore at the close of this chapter.

Parameters for Using AAE

At first glance, what is most striking about the Detroit students' assigned writings is the almost total absence of AAE. In 42 pieces of assigned writing sent electronically to the UM tutors by 17 different students, I found very few instances of AAE: an absent copula and one multiple negation, and both instances occurred in directly quoted dialogue. The e-mail conversations of participating dyads likewise show little or no evidence of AAE. Yet, all the Detroit students spoke AAE fluently. During the first year that I made regular visits to the school, I often heard teachers berate students for using AAE, admonishing them that they would never succeed in life or get jobs "talking like that." After teachers and students came to know me, however, teachers generally allowed students to speak AAE in my presence, only occasionally "correcting" students' use of AAE to SAE.[10] Why, then, does AAE not turn up in the electronic record?

True enough, both AAE and SAE are oral languages, while Edited American English (EAE) is a written language. So the conspicuous absence of AAE, an oral language, and the obvious code-switch to EAE, a written one, might be explained as an automatic switch from oral to written discourse, a choice largely driven by the medium (Victor Villanueva, personal communication, June 26, 2003). Transcribing AAE may be fraught with difficulty, but only because of its phonological distinctions, not because of its lexical and grammatical features, which are easy enough to write down. I maintain that code-switching between AAE and SAE—and its close kin EAE—is also highly sensitive to context, and the immediacy of e-mail makes that context even more complex. Although AAE is generally marked by lexical, grammatical, and phonological features, its oral use—and, I would add, its written use—is mainly defined by the speaker's relationship to the audience, if that speaker, first of all, has enough experience with code-switching (Baugh, 1983).

Knowing how and when to code-shift demonstrates one's verbal abilities, largely acquired through expanded social contacts. An expanded social network implicitly speaks to a person's experiential range and social sophistication. Children might speak AAE exclusively at home, but as they expand their social networks outside the home—to the playground, school, church, and job—so their stylistic range will expand. And as adults move into other situational contexts that might stigmatize AAE or even just stigmatize certain aspects of AAE more than others, such as the use of multiple negation, they learn to modify their speech in highly nuanced ways. Thus AAE is reserved not only for certain relationships but also for certain situations. Notably, these situations are not defined by race nor by the formality of the occasion; rather, they are defined by the familiarity between speaker and audience who share, or who do not share, knowledge of African American (AA) expressive culture (Baugh, 1983), or what I will refer to as insider-outsider status of the speaker relative to the audience.

This status affects the speaker's decision to use certain features of AAE or not to use it at all. Basically, four types of speaker-audience relationships are possible with the two variables that define insider-outsider status (degree of affiliation and knowledge of AAE expressive culture). Baugh's (1983) classification of these four types, which I have modified in insider–outsider terms, is as follows:

Type 1. Long-time friends who are natives of AA expressive culture; familiar insiders

Type 2. New acquaintances who are natives of AA expressive culture; unfamiliar insiders

Type 3. Familiar outsiders, such as school teachers and shopkeepers, with whom the speaker may or may not feel solidarity

Type 4. Unfamiliar outsiders, who might also hold more power than the speaker

Type 4 interactions might occur in a courtroom, for example, where use of AAE might signify hostile, aggressive intent, or at least resistance to and disrespect for authority. In sum, speakers are most likely to use AAE in a Type 1 situation; they are least likely to use it in a Type 4 situation.[11]

Even though a significant percentage of African Americans (80 percent in the early 1970s, according to Dillard, 1972) may be native speakers of AAE, not all native speakers are equally adept at all stylistic registers, such as city rap, country talk, fancy talk, or sweet talk, or with all the speech events within the larger AA rhetorical tradition. Nor would such expertise be appropriate for all native AAE speakers. Stylistic registers and speech events are also particular to a speaker's primary identification within a community. For example, playing the dozens is almost always reserved for familiar males on the street, whereas the maternal fuss is a female version of telling someone off, performed sometimes in public but most often in the home (Abrahams, 1976). In like manner, someone who wanted to be identified with street values could use street speech to make that identification known.

As these examples should also suggest, one other contextual factor plays a key role in the implicit rules for style-shifting: social domain. While native AAE speakers acquire their stylistic range as they move from the home, the playground, the job, and so forth, other social domains also have their preferred styles, most notably, the church and school in direct contradistinction to the street. Church and school closely align with the values represented by home: to wit, respectability, sensibility, family, and by extension, the social order. Street life stands in opposition to these values. All these domains are characterized by use of AAE, but home, street, and church and school have their respective stylistic registers. Traditionally, the home, church, and school are viewed as female institutions; all tend to place high value on speech making and oratory, and SAE is most often the prestige dialect (Abrahams, 1976). Of these institutions, the black church is most responsible for sustaining cultural membership and group identity. More important, church association is directly correlated to high school completion; it plays a more critical role in students' staying in school than family income or parents' education level (Heath, 1990).

Certainly, that was the case with the Detroit students, almost all of whom were avid churchgoers. In sum, the Detroit students, as churchgoers sharing information with outsiders via e-mail, within the social domain of school, would be decidedly disinclined to use AAE. Further, the school actively and specifically forbade students to play the dozens or to perform rap, because these speech events were associated with street culture.[12]

Writing for a Proximal Audience

It is precisely this highly situational use of AAE that makes it so difficult to study in cross-cultural communication with outsiders, however familiar: presumably one cannot study what is not there. As Baugh (1983) points out, "the very social isolation that is required to maintain linguistic (dialect) differences, to say nothing of the corresponding linguistic attitudes and stereotypes, is the very kind of isolation that causes street speakers to play hide-and-seek with their vernacular styles" (p. 93). Examining the Detroit students' papers now from the perspective of sociolinguistics, one can catch fleeting glimpses of African American expressive culture as students nonetheless engaged in the more subtle forms of style-shifting to meet the demands of contacts with outsiders within the domain of school and within the context of private e-mail, which they viewed as public communication.

One case in point: Jahidi (a pseudonym) sent the following paper to me privately via e-mail after the project was over just to practice his newly acquired skill in sending e-mail. It provides one of the clearest examples of a young writer working out the complex nuances of style-shifting, as he describes a confrontation on the basketball court in the context of a school paper to a familiar outsider (i.e., me).

Back In The Day

Two years ago it was me and my neighborhood friends, we decided to get the basketball games started. It was about one o'clock, when

we started to get the basketball games rollin. See people in my neighborhood take basketball real serious especicallay when your team is
losing. But in this case my friend Monte had a losing team and he
was also getting frustrated, so the person that was on my team
named David, decided to spark the game up with a little bit of trash
talking. Out of no where everyone started playing the game of basketball out of hate.

Me being the person I am I tried to bring everything to order by
saying, "hey everbody this is basketball not football, and plus we are
all friends so lets continue to play as if we all were winning." After
that we all continued to play the game of true basketball. We must
of played for about four of five hours straight, and that's what the
game is all about. A

Jahidi breaks off abruptly, probably because the class period ended, and
he had to leave the computer lab. Lack of time, too, may have been the
reason why the writer has to cut out detail. But notice that he has time to
tell me his friends' names and to directly quote his mediation of the brew-
ing conflict.

What Jahidi chooses to include and not include in this short piece is
significant. He reports that the group engaged in a round of trash talk, but
does not quote that talk. On the other hand, Jahidi's first person point of
view houses this narration in a stylistic register associated with that of the
black church, a homiletic tradition that conjoins the sacred and the mundane (Balester, 1993; Smitherman, 1977). Notice how Jahidi combines
plain talk, often colloquial (e.g., "we started to get the basketball games
rollin"; "David . . . decided to spark the game up"), with moral observations (e.g., "everyone started playing the game of basketball out of hate";
"we all continued to play the game of true basketball"; "this is basketball
not football"). Other papers sent to the UM tutors also elided describing
speech events in any detail. These elisions always occur in their personal
narrative papers, like Jahidi's, where the Detroit students *record* incidental
dialogue but only *report* climatic dialogue. At those moments in their narratives, they resort to indirect quotation when that dialogue enacts a speech
event associated with street culture or when the language code of that dialogue is most probably AAE, spoken among familiars.

Although certain topics are generally taken up in certain stylistic registers, a speaker may affect a particular style for a particular topic. That
personal choice reflects the speaker's verbal inventiveness (Baugh, 1983).
Matching style with topic can be orchestrated for serious or comic effect.
In the following example, Elvin (a pseudonym) employs a style that bears
comparison with the homiletic tradition of the black church, but the topic
under discussion is unexpectedly his short but happy life as a thief.

My Reflections

Before I was in the seventh grade, I used to steal from anyone I thought or knew had something I wanted. So I took what I want when I saw what I wanted it. I was a sly, cunning, and sneaky thief. I was caught only four times through my quick thieving career. It was a good life, but there was a down side to thieving. I had to keep my hands quick and my sense of my environment keen. I would steal from department stores with video cameras and dectors. I never got caught, but I came very close to being arrested.

I was with my grandmother when I almost got caught stealing from Toys 'R' Us. How did I almost get caught, the doors would not open for me. My grandmother thought I was not heavy enough to open the door but in actuality I had stolen something. So before security could come to check me I pushed open the door and walked out with my prize and a little extra, the sense of invincibility. Then after that I thought I could steal the world or even the universe. Most of the time I thought I could steal from my from my mother so one day I tried it. That was the first time I ever stole something from my mother or even stole some money. The feeling I got from stealing money made want to do it again and again. I first started stealing dollars, only ones. Then I decided to try big money (now everybody know back then one's, five's, and ten's were big money not like now a days). So one day after that I saw her purse open, I went through her purse and took five dollars.

I was never caught, but I do believe she that she knew I stole from her. Just me thinking that she knew from her made my body quiver and put a big smile on my face even though I knew I might get in trouble I still smiled. That was the main reason I stopper stealing from anyone ever again. I reflect on my criminal past and I think that I could have been a master criminal, even better than the best to date. This is my story and if you have a problem with this you keep it to yourself.

Elvin adroitly manipulates reader expectations throughout the piece, starting in the first paragraph where he seems to suggest that he used to be a thief but changed his ways because of its downside—"I had to keep my hands quick and my sense of my environment keen"—which is not the kind of downside that the reader expects. And in the last paragraph, Elvin sets up the reader to expect a statement of repentance, only to deliver the opposite: "Just me thinking that she knew [I stole] from her made my body quiver and put a big smile on my face." The word *thieving*, a more biblical-sounding word than *stealing*, is a lexical choice that rings true with the homiletic tradition. Significantly, the narrative is either a complete fiction or, at least, an embellished version of the truth, as inconsistencies in the tale itself (i.e., did he get caught four times or did he never get caught?) might suggest. Elvin was a devout churchgoer and generally a cooperative student, who nonetheless resisted participating in the online project with UM. When he did participate, he did so with a vengeance, as it were, choosing to manifest his resistance in a time-honored fashion of African American expressive culture: by signifying on his UM tutor, whom he supposes holds stereotypic views of him as a thief.

Further, in sending his thief story to an outsider via e-mail, Elvin tested the privacy of e-mail, as the last line of his essay seems to suggest: "This is my story and if you have a problem with this you keep it to yourself." He would have been severely reprimanded for sending his thief story if his teachers had known, but even so, he would have gained respect with some of his peers, for "talking bad," a kind of street talk, with its characteristic topics of violence, drugs, and other criminal activities, that carries covert prestige with young people, especially young men. Conceivably, Elvin may have shared his thieving essay with select peers for this reason. Thus Elvin's act of resistance cut at least two ways: it signified on white stereotypes of young African American males; but it also subverted the school's concerted efforts to control its public image on Front Street. While it might be argued that most young men, not just African Americans, enjoy "talking bad," this kind of talk among young African American males is especially pernicious, for it always runs the risk of perpetrating stereotypes that, in turn, too often have life-or-death consequences for young African American males.

Another student, Reuben (a pseudonym), used much the same strategy but with very different results. Reuben's tale came in response to an assignment that asked students to explain a process that they knew well. In his first draft attempt for this assignment, Reuben chose to describe how to smoke crack. But his teacher refused to accept the paper on grounds that this student, whom she described to me as a "good kid" in the community, had in fact no first-hand knowledge of this process and therefore could not write on the topic. He was "talking junk," the teacher told me, as she recounted events in Reuben's attempts to do this process-paper assignment.

In his second attempt, he explained how to roll a joint. This draft was rejected on the same grounds. At that point in time, the student's mother heard "through the grapevine," in the teacher's words, about Reuben's two draft attempts. His mother then showed up unexpectedly in class and upbraided him for "putting that kind of business on Front Street," as the teacher reported the mother's words to me. Finally, his third draft attempt was accepted—this time, on how to repair a bicycle tire—although he did not own a bicycle and probably never had, the teacher told me as she smiled and shook her head.[13] Reuben's first two drafts about drugs might be read as acts of resistance, signifying on stereotypes of African American city youth. His third draft about repairing a bicycle tire, although it too belied the writer's firsthand knowledge according to his teacher, was nonetheless an acceptable public view of the community's life.

Although most of the topics that the Detroit students wrote about did have potential relevance to students' lived experiences and thus lent themselves to vivifying detail, the papers that resulted from these topics actually held very little verisimilitude. For example, many students wrote about how to perform the Heimlich maneuver in a restaurant setting, a circumstance that could not have been as common in students' lives as these papers would suggest. While the Heimlich maneuver papers were assigned specifically by their teachers, students also wrote process papers on other topics that they self-selected. For example, several female students wrote their process papers on how to do a manicure. Nail art, not just nail care, was a topic on which they all had special expertise, for they took great pride and spent much time on creating exquisitely painted, decorated, and detailed nails. Yet none of their papers broached the topic beyond generic knowledge of manicuring that even a nail biter would know. Only one paper in its opening paragraph hints at the importance of nails to the writer's self-presentation:

How to take care of your nails

Taking care of your nails is a simple technique that requires time and concentration. When doing nails you are also thinking about how you will present yourself to others. Your nails can tell a lot about you. Short nails tell people that you are active in sports or some kind of recreation activity. If your nails are chewed up or rough this sometimes tell people that you are nervous or afraid. Long nails tell people that you have nails are healthy and you spend time on your nails. . . .

Writing for a Distant Audience

Interestingly, the students included more revealing papers in their ACT portfolios, which were sent to Iowa City for scoring. These papers were never sent to their UM tutors. For example, Ruthie (a pseudonym) sent several pieces to her UM tutor but did not send him the paper she wrote for the so-called "thesis statement paper" required for the ACT portfolio.

After the class had read Arthur Miller's *The Crucible*, students were to write about the problem of mob rule in the play and in two other instances from real life. For Ruthie's two real-life examples, she wrote of the Rodney King riots and of a riot that took place at the school that year when security guards chained the doors to the school to prevent tardy students from entering the building. According to Ruthie's description, the frustrated students crashed through the doors somehow, overturned the metal detector thresholds, and scuffled with the security people. Absent from her description were details (a deficit uncharacteristic of her other work)—details like who and how many persons were involved and what disciplinary action was taken afterwards. But such details could have incriminated people with whom she felt affiliation. She did not send the piece to her UM tutor, probably she did not want to trash-talk her school with an outsider; but she sent it to ACT for it was safe to do so, but without details that her teachers might read and report.

Ruthie's decisions on what to send to Iowa City and what to send to Ann Arbor suggests she was very aware of relative distances. She chose not to disseminate information to a proximal audience, information that might have a negative impact on community members or might present a negative picture of the community, especially to another nearby community. Kochman (1981) points out that census takers often have difficulty getting data in central cities, even when the census takers are African American. I would add that residents wrongly suspect that personal household information might be used against them, even though it is also used for other purposes, such as ascertaining political representation and federal funds for the larger community. Nonetheless, the personal consequences, those closest to home—at once, economic, political, and social—may be too great to bear when heaped on the other hardships of people's lives.

The following is another example of a paper that illustrates how information might be too dangerous to divulge locally, but not at a distance. In this paper sent to Iowa City but not to Ann Arbor, the writer shares a reminiscence of a murder in the family. The sketchiness and inconsistencies in the narrative give it a nightmarish quality:

2:00 a.m. At the Hospital

It was the summer of 1989. Everyone was in the bed sleeping. The phone rang at about 1:30 that morning. It was my aunty calling and saying "Darwin in the hospital, get to the hospital, we don't know if he gone make it." My mother woke me up and we went to the hospital.

When we arrived at Receiving Hospital, my family was screaming and crying. The doctor came out and said that he's not going to make it. My grandmother and mother stood in the emergency room watching my cousin Darwin die slowly. Seconds later his body started shaking and blood gushed out of his mouth. My mother ran out in tears screaming "he's gone!" Nurses tried to get my grandmother out of the room. Darwin died. When the doctor told everyone they started to cry and yell at the doctor.

Darwin had been beaten with a steel bat and stabbed in the head several times. The doctor did tell us that he fought for his life. My aunty, his mother admitted stabbing him, but she said she didn't beat him.

When my aunty stabbed Darwin in the hand she panicked and immediately ran out the back door to the gas station to call the police. At that time someone else went through the front door and started beating Darwin with a steel bat. I don't know why anyone would do something like that to him because he was loved by everyone. If my aunty hadn't run out the house he probably would've beat her too.

Months later my aunty bought a Ouija board and everyone was sitting around asking the Ouija board questions about the murder. At first, we were a little confused. But it did tell us that my aunty didn't beat him, it was someone else in the area. When we went to court we learned that the Ouija board was right. My aunty served two months maybe more and was released. The man at the gas station witnessed her running to the phone booth with a knife in her hand and verified her story.

This incident has made me look at people a different way. You can't trust anyone, not even your mother. When I think back to things like that, it makes me wonder about my aunty. Even though the courts said she didn't kill her son I feel she did kill him, because she stabbed him and that was enough to kill a person. If she killed her own son, who's to say she won't kill me?

I do not like going around my aunty. Because when she gets drunk she gets crazy, upset, and she starts hollering. Once she threw me into a wall because she was upset that it was taking my mother a long time to get back to pick me up.

Why do people act that way towards the ones they love? People say "blood is thicker than water." But I don't think it really matters because people often hurt the ones they love. I've learned that you can't get upset with someone and take their life away because some-

thing didn't go the way you planned. I guess there is a thin line between love and hate.

COMPUTING ON FRONT STREET

The ACT portfolios also included the writing of many students who did
not participate in the online project with UM, either by choice or because
they were not in the selected group. When compared to the pieces sent
electronically to UM, the portfolio samples reveal a much wider range of
topics as well as a much lower range of writing ability. These samples also
present evidence of some of the more pronounced features of AAE, such as
multiple negation for emphasis. And most significant of all, they bear evidence of students' still emerging computing skills; for example, most students used extravagant fonts that rendered their texts almost unreadable,
a common practice among new users. Most of the pieces by students who
chose not to participate in the UM/Detroit project appear to be simply
underdeveloped, as in this example quoted in full:

Should student wear or not wear unionform

Why student should not wear unionform cause it's not changing anything the student stell wear there own cloths if they wont to. One of
the reasons why they said student should wear unionforms cause
they might get shot or killed over the type of cloths they wear. Students should wear unionform if the parents tell them to.
Students should wear unionform if they can stay out of trouble.

I want to suggest, however, that all these features—the incidents of marked
AAE features, the wider range of topics, the lower range of writing ability
and computer skills—profile students who were less adept at style-shifting
and more linguistically isolated than the students who did choose to participate in the online project and who were, not coincidentally, the strongest
writers in the school.

Further, the computers both helped and hindered these students. On
the one hand, the computers were new writing tools that engaged students
and encouraged them to write; on the other, the computers separated the
females from the males, and the males from the boys, as it were. The female
students usually had keyboarding skills, but the male students did not. For
lack of keyboarding and computing skills, much of their work looked like
the "unionform" paper just cited. Although some male students did know
how to keyboard and may have had some computing experience in other

classes, almost all of them claimed to know how to send e-mail. In fact, no one (male or female) knew how to send e-mail. Writing within the time constraints of the class period on an unfamiliar instrument in an unstable network created too many opportunities for embarrassment on Front Street. How did students forestall that embarrassment? Most often, by refusing technical assistance and feigning to know all about computers, when in fact they did not even know where the power button was. Such were the signs of independence and pride from students who did not want help from an outsider and, at the same time, who wanted to manage their self-presentations before familiars on Front Street—in this case, the computer lab itself.

IMPLICATIONS FOR TEACHING

The UM/Detroit project represents the kind of cross-cultural interaction that we might expect between these two sets of students from institutions on opposite sides of the digital divide. It also holds important implications for teachers working with African American students, whether they work together online or in the classroom. Recognizing that African American expressive culture is neither monolithic nor static, English educators none-theless must be aware of race-based cultural differences in information sharing and AAE use as they design their curricula, structure their pedagogical choices, and reconsider assessment issues.

First of all, African American students' writing may look much like that produced by basic writers, regardless of ethnicity or gender. The two most prominent writing issues in the papers of the Detroit students—lack of development and verb tense shifts—are two areas that give most basic writers difficulty. A paper's short length, as we saw in "Should students wear or not wear unionform," not only marks lack of idea development but also lack of *fluency*, most simply defined as the ability to produce words on paper. This deficit of detail accounts for the high-context, writer-centered quality of basic writers' prose, including that produced by the Detroit students, as we saw in "2 a.m. at the Hospital" and "Back in the Day."

Verb tense shifts often create problems, it seems, with writers working primarily from oral traditions, not just African American basic writers. Shifting into present tense when summarizing and analyzing literature is a difficulty encountered even by college writers in entry-level courses. The prose style of African American high school students is marked by narrative interspersion and circumlocution (Ball, 1992), characteristics that might create the verb tense difficulties in the papers from the Detroit students. But other students working primarily from oral traditions rather than written ones, including low-SES white students from the South, for example, are also very adept at narrative interspersion and circumlocution and may have similar difficulty in shifting into appropriate verb tenses.

But here is the key difference between African American student writers and basic writers generally: the challenge is doubly difficult for African American students if they are also deeply conflicted about whether or not to record or to report speech events that are generally disallowed expression in the domain of school. The temptation to use direct quotations rather than indirect quotations might also be linked to a cultural value on public performance. Writers have to decide not only what to re-create but also how to re-create these scenes from real life into academic writing. These kinds of rhetorical decisions might exacerbate African American students' sense of double consciousness, where home, street, and school literacies go head-to-head.

Thus the primary difference between the writing produced by basic writers generally and by African American basic writers more specifically is not so much in kind but in degree. That degree makes all the difference in the world, for the stakes are simply much higher for African American students than for white students and their respective futures. A young white male in a job interview might not be well-spoken or may speak a variety of English common to the South, which may even sound very much like AAE, or may just sound "country"—and not get a job because his language use is stigmatized.[14] But the next young white male who comes in for an interview will not be prejudged as ignorant or mentally deficit and will still be given a chance to create his own impression with the prospective employer. On the other hand, a young African American male will more likely be prejudged as ignorant or worse, before he opens his mouth. Even if he does not speak AAE in the job interview, his positive impression will not change the situation for the next young African American male who interviews with this employer. And if he does speak AAE in the job interview? His example will reflect not only on himself but also on his whole community, and damning stereotypes will continue to dominate employers' attitudes.[15]

Unfortunately, being able to speak SAE and to write EAE is no guarantee of social mobility, but without these literacy skills, individuals can perpetrate stereotypes that will continue to dog African Americans as a group. To be sure, everyone must learn that a certain species of talk is appropriate for different places and with different audiences. Actually, SAE has a much narrower range than AAE. Nonetheless, a native AAE speaker who already has a wide rhetorical repertoire must learn yet another variety of English—SAE—as she expands her contacts in social domains outside the home.

Learning to edit grammatical features of AAE to conform to the grammatical features of EAE is the easy part, if the papers from the Detroit students are any indication. Far more difficult is mastering the conventions of the written word, especially now that the preferred writing technology today, the computer, is so much more difficult to operate than previous dominant writing technologies, that is, pen and paper. Computers are far less affordable to African Americans living in central cities than are pen and paper. And Internet-connected computers' capability to replicate and disseminate text-based information make this writing technology more threatening than pen and paper for a community that so cautiously guards its business on Front Street.

Because native speakers of AAE may be acquiring new competencies in yet more varieties of English (SAE and EAE) and may be using computers for the first time, tutors and teachers might expect to see more errors in grammar and mechanics and from students at a later age in central city schools (depending on how linguistically isolated the community is) than from basic writers in other school settings. This increased error rate at a later age will make it *appear* that African American students are ignorant or even intellectually deficit. And that perception, especially in the classroom, not only hinders learning, it also perpetrates pernicious stereotypes, which can become self-fulfilling prophecies. Young African American writers must also contend with other social pressures that stigmatize succeeding in school and using EAE as "writing white," which is one step toward "acting white."

How then should tutors and teachers approach the intensive but necessary work on the conventions of EAE? Certain teaching strategies can be worse than ineffective, for they fail to take into account culture and history. Certain methods, too, assume certain linguistic and computing competencies, such as "read your paper aloud to see if everything sounds right" or "be sure to use your spell-checker feature of your word processor." For example, one student in his ACT portfolio consistently spelled *and* as *an*, thus retaining a phonological feature often associated with AAE, a spelling that would not have shown up as incorrect on spell-checker and a pronunciation that would have sounded right to the writer. Obviously, the writer has never seen or noticed the spelling of *and* in writing. Small wonder in this particular school setting, where almost all the literature is read aloud because there are not enough books for a whole class, much less enough to allow students to take them home to read.

The best strategy is to identify the pattern of error, one or two patterns at a time, a pedagogy advanced by Mina Shaughnessy (1977). But in the context of a classroom of students with a nonwhite or low-SES majority, the pattern will likely be shared across the group. Literacy development is not that individualistic, although every individual will exhibit certain idiosyncrasies in her writing. More likely, the writing of most individuals will share common points of competencies as well as incompetencies. These commonalities derive in part from attending the same school and experiencing the same curriculum and pedagogy. At the time of the project, most teachers at Detroit High School assigned very little writing, and thus most students had very little experience with school writing. Because they have similar schooling, their collective literacy development *as a group* travels much the same arc. These common patterns of error also derive from a shared oral language learned at home and in the neighborhood. So, for example, with the Detroit students' papers, several had difficulties with shifting tense when framing and relating a narrative. This pattern might be productively addressed as a group, with discussion of why so many have the same difficulty at this particular juncture in their narratives. That discussion might, at the same time, involve talking about what business can be appropriately put on Front Street without fronting or betraying the writer, her home, or her community.

Or not. For it would be dangerous to assume that African American students generally are all native speakers of AAE or even that most share a knowledge of African American expressive culture, with a common felt sense of what is or is not appropriate in a particular context. Knowledge of African American expressive culture is not necessarily valued among all African Americans. Many middle-class African Americans, for example, are appalled by the street speech valorized in gangsta rap and even the blues (B. Monroe, 1994). While such class differences within the African American community have often been noted, even within one stratum of socioeconomic class, native speakers of AAE speak different varieties of AAE governed by different rules of style-shifting. These different varieties arise in very different urban and rural contexts, which in turn have very different local histories and agendas vis-à-vis mainstream cultures. Thus Kochman's formulations are based on African American communities in Chicago; Abrahams's, in Philadelphia, Texas, and the Caribbean; and Heath's, in the Carolina Piedmonts. And as Heath's later work astutely established, these multiple Englishes and linguistic behaviors can become quickly diluted when native speakers move into other regions, other cities— even other forms of architecture, such as high-rise housing projects—and other ways of life (Heath, 1990).

English teachers need always to be aware, too, of race-based cultural differences when designing their curricula. Using rap music in the classroom, even "positive" rap music, as has been done successfully (but notably, not without controversy) in Chicago schools (Mahiri, 1998), for example, would not be allowed at Detroit High School, which expressly banned street culture in the classroom. Because of its association with street culture and because of its sexually explicit lyrics, rap music poses problems for many churchgoing African Americans, especially among the middle-class, who want to distance themselves from this musical genre, as well as the earlier blues tradition that celebrated women's sexuality (Gates, 1990; Monroe, 1994).

While topical and lexical appropriateness sharply diverge between the classroom and the street, other features of street culture may be productively appropriated in the English classroom. Many of the speech events associated with the street—especially on the playground, for example, as we have seen in Jahidi's paper—might be expressed within the context of academic writing, where vivifying detail is positively valued in genres such as the personal narrative. In fact, this dialogue needs to be directly quoted and reproduced not just to realize the full effect of the story but also to appreciate the writer's linguistic competence and for the writer himself to appreciate this as a linguistic competence not everyone possesses. The writer can take pride in a rich rhetorical tradition that is so closely associated with a group's linguistic identity historically.

These performances in writing, as it were, also help preserve these traditions. I would also suggest that the dialogue of speech events, when directly recorded in academic work, should be topically and lexically true to form, thereby demonstrating to students that "appropriateness" is not a static absolute. Rather, it is usually defined by white, middle-class standards of conversation etiquette and home literacies, standards that also, not coincidentally, dominate classrooms and academic writing. The disconnect between home and school literacies for native speakers of AAE (and speakers of other varieties of English, for that matter) can be ameliorated by giving students permission to demonstrate linguistic competencies of their home literacies in school too. Allowing them to make these connections may also blur the direct line between succeeding in school and "acting white." Succeeding in school should not have to mean just "acting white" but also "talking black."

Minimally, teachers and tutors need to be able to recognize when native speakers of AAE are working within the homiletic stylistic register. Failing to do so, English educators may miss a chance to build on students' linguistic strengths; worse, they may do irreparable damage to students' writing development. As we have seen in Elvin's piece on thieving, this style is marked by use of homilies, simple and compound sentence syntax consistent with oral delivery, mixed diction, word or phrase repetitions, and subtle humor and irony, often in the form of signifying. Traditional writing instruction too often calls for drilling students on doing just the opposite—that is, combining sentences into complex ones, explaining abstract ideas literally, making literal lexical choices, varying word choice to avoid repetition, and achieving a neutral, objective voice devoid of humor, so as not to compromise the writer's ethos and credibility in academic writing. We need to understand, however, how to recognize the homiletic tradition within the classroom in order to appropriate its strengths to build competence in academic writing. This issue is not so much a curricular issue as it is a pedagogical one, largely in the way teachers and tutors provide feedback and assess students' work.

Although the UM tutor's response to Elvin's piece on thieving did not survive, Elvin was pleased with her response. The UM tutor apparently appreciated the piece, for he wrote back:

> Hey Margaret [a pseudonym],
> I like your idea of talking a little more about the ups and downs of theiving. Thank you for the compliment about how I made a good combination of seriousness and humor . . .

In like manner, teachers should not penalize students for making the complex connections between the sacred and mundane that mark the homiletic tradition; on the contrary, I want to suggest that teachers should make these connections explicit. If and when such features appear in concert in student writing, the tradition should be discussed as a distinctive rhetoric, one not confined to the black church and the evangelical tradition, but one that has also found much currency in the Civil Rights movement and politics more generally, although in diluted or hybrid forms. Talking explicitly of the rhetorical features of the homiletic tradition will make students more generally aware of writing as dynamic, relative to audience, purpose, and place. It will also make students aware that these writing decisions are not necessarily individualistic but rather have certain patterns and rhetorical histories. In other words, teachers should seize the opportunity to reinstate culture and history into language use.

Appreciating the homiletic tradition, of course, might also have a curricular dimension, if examples such as Martin Luther King, Jr.'s speeches are actually studied and compared to, say, Johnnie Cochran's closing argument in the O. J. Simpson trial (Walker, 2003). Or even just examining speeches from a current political campaign could be a productive lesson in language as well as an example of critical pedagogy, focusing on making connections between school and the real world preparatory to taking action.

Besides issues revolving around appropriate classroom application of rap and of the homiletic tradition, other curricular and pedagogical choices also loom large in the African American–majority classroom. These issues hold implications for classrooms with other cultural majorities as well. Asking students to write on any topic of their own choosing, or asking students to write personal narratives, or asking students to write about what they have firsthand knowledge of, or asking students to transform private journal writing to public writing—all of these standard assignments pose distinct problems for native speakers of AAE as well as members of many other American minority groups. For these kinds of writing assignments place inordinate value on the expressive purpose of writing as self-discovery and self-expression. When teachers insist that personal narrative especially should accurately reflect "true" lived experiences, they are partaking of a long tradition of institutional confession, in Foucault's words, "a ritual that unfolds within a power relationship, for one does not confess without the presence (or virtual presence) of a partner who is not simply the interlocutor but the authority who requires the confession, prescribes and appreciates it, and intervenes" (quoted in Faigley, 1992, p. 130).

This expressive, private-to-public writing model in secondary classrooms generally also drives assessment criteria when vivifying detail and "voice" count for "good writing." Such evaluative criteria fail to take notice that the value of self-disclosure is variously constrained by differences in cultures, classes, and genders, as we have seen in the UM/Detroit project. As Faigley (1992) stresses, "Those who encourage 'authentic voices,' in student writing often speak of giving students 'ownership' of a text or empowering students. The latter notion sounds like something all teachers would support (for who among us would 'disempower' students?), but it avoids the question of how exactly teachers are to give students power. Is it in self-expression or is it in earning power?" (p. 131). If teachers want students to empower themselves, they should give students the power and permission to "tell stories" and even "talk junk"—that is, to fictionalize autobiographically based writing. Such a pedagogical move disavows the notion of the unified, bourgeois self that implicitly undergirds the expressive model of writing instruction in the first place; such a move also grants students the power to construct and control their own self-presentations on Front Street.

This power of self-invention and self-fashioning is even more important when students are sharing work online than when they are working on paper. Although paper can be easily shared in small-group peer reviews, for example, the easy dissemination of e-mail or electronic postings to a class group are much more public. In electronic environments, authority resides not only with the teacher but also potentially with many peer readers, a shared authority not so much dispersed and diluted as it is multiplied and intensified (Faigley, 1992). This peer pressure can be used to positively support a culturally sensitive writing curriculum, one that does *not* ask students to necessarily write truly and factually about their lived experiences.

"Private e-mail" is quickly becoming an oxymoron in the early 2000s. As we increasingly become an epistolary society, we are learning from experience that hard drives can be legally seized, and e-mail messages can be too easily forwarded and disseminated to make them secure communication. The simplest solution is one that Emily Post advocated almost a century ago: She cautioned young women, whose reputations were especially precious and precarious on the marriage market, to never write in a private note what they would not want to see published on the front page of a newspaper. It is a rule of etiquette that the Detroit students certainly lived by. The UM tutors' insistence in 1996 that their e-mail conversations were personal and therefore private now seems naive, even quaint; the Detroit students' understanding of the medium as public has proven prescient by comparison.

Actually, making *all* classroom writing public—as if it were indeed the front page of a newspaper—would be more culturally relevant in the African American–majority classroom than trying to keep writing private. Going public could certainly be done via paper publication, but electronic publication is more thorough in that everything can be made public more easily and more widely, because it can reach so many more readers than paper publication. Electronic writing is also more immediate and therefore more performative in a way, because the writer is more clearly playing to a real audience, who can respond in kind. Besides intraclass and interclass communication via electronic media, teachers should also seek to make connections outside the classroom to the community and, ultimately, outside the community, perhaps to schools that serve students of a very different socioeconomic class. The point of these outside communications would be to break the linguistic isolation that so often characterizes the lives of students in high-poverty schools, but especially those schools in economically isolated areas like inner cities and remote reservations. Perhaps most important of all, text-based, faceless electronic interaction with out-groups heightens one's sense of group identity while it diminishes individual identity. This shift in subjectivity might help reconcile the contradictory consciousness so many students of color bring to the assimilationist classroom.

That classroom is too often dominated by individualist pedagogies. Solo performance and competitive learning are deeply alienating to many American minority groups, including African Americans, Latino Americans, and American Indians. These groups have historically valued learning from peers and from adults, in apprenticeship or by demonstrations, as in Reuben's paper, "How to Fix a Bike Tire," which begins: "my grandfather taught me how to fix a flat tire on a bike. He made it seem easy as I watched him demonstrate." Cooperative learning among peers closely aligns with collectivist notions of learning. Thus electronic networking does not represent much of a stretch for minority students already accustomed to vast social networks that not only disseminate information on Front Street but also have managed to maintain cultural knowledge for generations predominately through oral networks.

Unfortunately, formal schooling is largely grounded in the language socialization patterns of mainstream children, that is, the verbal display of knowledge and extended discourse forms centered on "chronicity and individuals as agents" (Heath, 1989, p. 347). Those patterns, however, do not hold true for most children of color and actually work against the values their communities hold dear, a point I will return to in detail in Chapter 4. Collaborative learning understood as reciprocal teaching is one classroom strategy that honors certain nonmainstream ways of being and believing and learning.

Indeed, the principles of coteaching are finding their way into American corporate life: individuals playing roles in teams, with power more evenly distributed across the group. Schooling now needs to follow suit.

CHAPTER 3

Crucible for Critical Literacy

What happens when the "have-nots" do have access to Internet-connected computers and then participate in a Web-based discussion about freedom and justice—not with "haves" but with other "have-nots"? To what degree can they use communication technology to foster critical literacy among themselves?

This chapter seeks to explore these questions, taking a close look at one online project that connected two high-poverty schools with different cultural majorities: one, Latino of Mexican descent and, the other, Plateau Indian. (I will leave the tribe unspecified in an effort to protect the anonymity of the schools.) The communities that these two schools serve hold diametrically opposing political views on volatile regional issues. Further, the two cultural majorities in question have distinctly different histories vis-à-vis El Hombre/The White Man, as voluntary immigrants and as an involuntary minority, respectively. Their futures, however, seem ordained to converge on the same path, as both groups will likely experience job discrimination, political invisibility, and cultural erosion and loss.

An examination of the transcript generated from these two schools' interaction online should suggest that other kinds of divides deserve our attention—not just the divide between rich and poor but also the divide between communities of "have-nots," too often portrayed as an undifferentiated mass in the public discourse on the digital divide. For these populations in particular, a critical literacy education might truly alter their futures as individuals and, conceivably, as communities. I maintain that communication technology holds transformative potential for the disenfranchised, the children of immigrants and indigenous peoples alike, but only when technology is coupled with a critical pedagogy. Having either, much less both, presents serious challenge in high-poverty schools, where teachers struggle with inadequate access and suffer considerable pressure to focus strictly on basic skills.

LOCAL CONTEXTS

Yet some teachers remain undaunted. In the fall of 2000, two such teachers from two different schools—Garland High School and Tribal School (both pseudonyms)—brought their students together for a Web-based threaded discussion over the course of a 2-month period. The two teachers designed and implemented the project themselves; they graciously allowed me to examine the electronic record long after the project was over. What made this online project remarkable, among other reasons, was that it took place between two schools serving working-class communities, so close geographically—only about 75 miles apart—but worlds apart culturally and politically.

Both schools serve predominately poor populations. A multiethnic town, Garland has a Latino majority (56%), with 37% white, 2.9% African American, 1.8% Asian/Pacific American, and 0.5% Native American (tribes unspecified) (U.S. Census Bureau, 2000). Most residents are employed in the agriculture industry, although three large food-processing plants have diversified Garland's economy in the past decade. The high school, the second largest in the state with 2,200–2,400 students, serves free or reduced lunch for 80% of its students. A small percentage of students, predominately white, are relatively well off, their parents employed as white-collar workers in scientific fields in a nearby town, as management employees at the food-processing plants, or as large tract farmers around Garland.[1]

Tribal School is a small school of about 100 students in grades 7–12. In order to enroll, students must be enrolled members of a particular Plateau Indian tribe, although many also have other ethnic backgrounds, most commonly Latino of Mexican descent. Like all federally designated tribal schools, Tribal School offers a culturally relevant curriculum, including Plateau Indian language study taught by community members and activities such as berry picking and root digging. Typically, Tribal School offers a place for students who have not succeeded in local public schools. All students at the school are served both breakfast and lunch. Most of the parents of these students are unemployed; those who are employed generally work for the tribe in some capacity.

The two teachers hoped that by connecting their respective schools electronically, socially, and intellectually, they would give their students an authentic learning experience, one where they would have to communicate with people other than their teachers. The teachers also wanted their students to have the opportunity to consider opposing political viewpoints, which in this case are largely based on cultural differences as well as economic survival. They decided to focus on a piece of literature common to their curricula, Arthur Miller's *The Crucible*. With that literature touchstone, they constructed three sets of questions for their students to discuss online, with an initial posting due one week and two responses to others posted the following week.

Three junior-level classes at Garland High School and one sophomore-level class at Tribal School participated. Of the 88 Garland students, 41 were Latino, 34 were white, 3 were African American, 3 were Asian American, and 2 were half American Indian of unspecified tribal origin. That breakdown is roughly representative of the demographics of the whole school. All of the 15 Tribal School students involved in the project were registered tribal members, which is requisite for enrollment. In the online environment, the Garland students were assigned to eight small groups with about 11 students in each group, drawn from different class periods. Three or four Tribal School students were assigned to four of those eight groups. Thus four groups were comprised strictly of Garland students; four had members from both schools.

The project took place over a 2-month period (minus Thanksgiving week) from November 1 to December 18, 2000. In all, students posted almost 1,200 messages, despite limited access and technical difficulties. The Garland students had access to a newly wired computer classroom, albeit in the elementary school annex, a 10-minute walk away. At Tribal School, the class had access to about four or five computers (depending on whether or not inoperable computers are counted), but not all of those were connected to the Internet; at times during the project, none of them was connected due to server problems. Although a new server was brought online in early December, connectivity to the school was intermittent at best for the duration of the project. The discussion prompts clustered around three assignments, all based on *The Crucible*. Certain questions, however, engaged students more dramatically than others. Those questions will be the focus of my analysis.

INTERCULTURAL CONTACT

Most of the discussion prompts centered on the issue of freedom and justice, then (in the time of the play) and now. Students from the two schools clearly do not share the same values, I would argue, because they do not share the same history. Although a few white and Latino students questioned the American justice system, the vast majority did not. In decided contrast, all Tribal School students doubted that freedom and justice are available to all.

These opposing beliefs on the justice system emerged when students were asked at the beginning of the 2-month discussion, "What do freedom and justice mean to you?" The Latino students' postings reveal a belief that the American system is just when compared to the justice systems in other countries that they have experienced, either directly or indirectly through their parents and grandparents: "Justice is something we have in this world. Like the police give us justice all the time. Mostly every one has freedom in america. Freedom is something everyone should have but that does not happen in every country."[2] At least one student contrasts the U.S. system with communism, a comment that ironically harkens back to the Red Scare rhetoric of the McCarthy era, which *The Crucible* implicitly critiques: "If we didn't get to make our own choices and decisions then we would just be like any communist country that the government runs everything we do (even what we watch, read, and believe)." Another Latino student ties the twin concepts of freedom and justice to economic opportunity: "freedom and justice are basically the same thing, it gives everyone equality and choices and chances in life." Yet another expresses even more explicitly the ideology of bootstraps: "It means to have the opportunity [to] succeed and to go through life without problems or worries."

Interestingly, a few Latina female students did not agree with this majority sentiment. But they seem to be critiquing not so much the justice system, but parental or perhaps spousal constraints on their movements:

> justice and freedom means the ability for myself to make choices. justice is being given the chance to explain yourself and not to get judged right off the bat for doing something. You have the right to tell your side of the story. freedom is the chance to be able to do what you want if it's not against the law. you have the ability to make choices for yourself and not allow someone to control your life.

Tribal School students openly challenged Garland students' belief in freedom and justice throughout the transcript on several occasions. For example, in response to a Latino student's posting, "justice and freedom two words that i hope are allways around," a Tribal School student writes:

> But what do thos words realy mean. You have said one thing but what does it realy mean do you think there is such a thing as freedom and justice because if you realy think about it is there justice for all that is the question. So even if thos words are around for a long time what will mean if you can't ever realy be free.

The subject line for the Tribal School student's posting is "I have a dream," an allusion to the Civil Rights movement, pointedly suggesting that the dream of freedom and justice has yet to be realized.

A related issue surfaces later in the discussion with this question posed by the teachers: "Salem become famous for its 'witch hunts.' Can you think of any modern day examples that are also considered witch hunts? What does this say about our society?" At Garland High School, many answered that there are no witch hunts now because there are no witches or because people do not believe in witches now (as opposed to then), or because witchcraft is no longer a crime. Others, clearly working from literal definitions and associations, cited as examples the Blair Witch Project, the electric chair, running after fugitives, Ouija boards, Easter egg hunts, serial killers, extraterrestrials, and the 2000 presidential election in Florida. However, at least one white student did understand the metaphoric meaning of a witch hunt, responding that hippies and "kids who look different" are targeted for scrutiny, especially since the Columbine High School tragedy. In the following example, another white student misunderstands the analogy and literalizes the question, but does make the connection between then and now:

> Another example is the hunt for the murder of a white woman in Boston in the 80's where black men were harassed and abused for the murder of this woman when her husband was the one who killed her.
> This play gives an example of how our society says that it has changed so much but in a sense it is still the same in many ways. There are still people being harassed for their color of their skin, nationality, or there religion. It is sad but true that we have not really came as far as we think we have.

Like this white student at Garland, Tribal School students spoke vehemently against the injustice of the death penalty; further, they consistently made connections between then and now. In the following exchange between a Tribal School student and a Latino student from Garland, we see that that the two students agree in principle, but the Latino student nonetheless disconnects then and now, the very connection the Tribal School student is trying to make:

> The people who were on death row and found inocent after they were put to sleep long time, the people that did it should've died with them so they can keep them company and something like that today it's a law suit or you get canned for not looking over the files carefully to see if he's inocent. . . . the play says that it's injustice and there is no freedom and if your guilty, your guilty until your hung. (Tribal School student)

Yes, I think your right. The people in Salem didn't really aks a lot or try to proof that your innocent. They wanted to get over with all this witchcraft and if someone in the court wasn't your friend you hang.

I'm very happy, that we don,t have the death penalty so much anymore. (Garland student)

Of the three sets of questions that fueled this intercultural discussion of *The Crucible*, one particular question seemed to ignite the most pointed, most specific responses from students from both schools: "How far would you go to fight for something you believe in?" The responses from the two schools most clearly contrast, respectively, their histories as children of voluntary immigrants and children of an involuntary minority, reduced in number and power through genocide and conquest. By far the most common response from Garland, students said they would die for their future families, with religion as the second most common response. In the following example, the student hopes her future family will have more control over their "outcomes" (or does she mean "income"?): "I would galdly die if I knew [my future husband and children] were going to live a life where they controlled thier outcome." Another student agrees with her, saying that she too would sacrifice freedom today to "know that my future family will be safe and living in a good world." Most of the Tribal School students, however, said they would fight to preserve their ancestral lands. One group, then, looked to the future; the other, to the birthright from their collective past.

Students' contrasting responses reflected not only on their futures and pasts but also on their presents. One Garland student—albeit only one student—raises the issue of the breaching the dams: "i would defintly fight for what i totaly believe in, like the dams because that has to do with the way we live and agriculture we need that to live." Several Tribal School students asserted that they would fight to save their reservation. Tribal School students also go on to explain how they would fight: by organizing and getting involved politically. One student writes, "I would go petty far or utill i win, or get close. i would never give up. like if i were fighting to keep our land i would get all our people involved because it's our land. thats all." Another explains how far she would go to save the reservation: "Far as finishing high school, getting a masters degree, and following that is running for a board member of my tribal council. That is how far I would go to save my land."

Thus in these few instances the two schools broach, however obliquely, the most volatile topics of the region: the breaching of the dams and the tribal termination movement. The tribal termination movement is backed by white supremacists, among other interest groups. This movement seeks

to terminate tribal status, and by extension, the reservation system altogether, which proponents see as the root of several problems, including
Indian casinos and water management. On the issue of the dams, Latinos
and Plateau Indian students would most certainly and heatedly disagree.
For their respective communities, the stakes are nothing short of economic
survival. To better understand these stakes, a little background is in order.

Arguably, the Plateau Indians are the most politically astute and active
tribe in the region. Although they ceded approximately 90% of their ancestral land to the United States government in the 1850s, they still retained
fish and wildlife harvesting rights. As early as the 1880s, the Plateau nation
started asserting its treaty rights, legally challenging water management
and fishing on rivers running through their ancestral lands (Hunn, 1990;
Ulrich, 1999). These challenges have generally been upheld by the federal
government against local and state claims to the contrary (Titone, 2000).
In the 1930s, New Deal projects spawned 15 dams across two major rivers
in the region (Hunn, 1990). While these dams irrigate over a half million
acres and provide hydroelectric power to over ten million residents, they
have also exterminated thousands of miles of salmon runs. The loss of the
fisheries also has religious ramifications for Plateau Indians, for they are
spiritually accountable as stewards of the land and its resources. Further,
loss of the fisheries has translated into deeper impoverishment of the reservation's subsistent economies, with unemployment rates rising to as high
as 80% in 2000 with decreasing annual catches, among other causes. An
estimated 30% of young fish are churned up by turbines at the dams each
year. Attempted solutions, such as fish ladders up the dams and fish barges
around the dams, have proven ineffective in restoring the upriver runs
(Hunn, 1990). The solution proposed now by environmental and Plateau
Indian groups is the breaching of these dams. But to do so, the opposing
side argues, would decimate the agricultural industry, which is totally dependent on irrigation from the rivers. And the large Latino immigrant population in the region, who work the fields, stand to lose their major source
of employment if these dams are breached.

At several points in the electronic transcripts, then, we see two divergent world orientations, economic, cultural, and historical at the same
time. One orientation looks to the future, holding to the bootstraps notion
of improving future generations' lot, if not one's own; the other remembers
and respects the past, holding on to ancestral land and the values it represents: collectivity and collective action.

Although students between the two schools did not respond to, much
less sustain, discussion on key issues dividing them politically, some Garland students did challenge their peers to dig deeper from time to time
throughout the 2-month period. Theirs was not the majority opinion. Still,

they did question the unquestioned, did measure nationalistic abstractions against their own lived experience, did attempt to resituate and denaturalize received knowledge. These moments of resistance, taken together, bear witness to students' unpacking the logic of capitalism that promises to raise the lot of the poor even as it keeps them in their place—in this case, in the fields as day laborers or on the welfare rolls as the unemployed.

The electronic record bears witness to many such moments. While most Latino students felt lucky to be able to "vote for our leaders" which in turn ensures that "we can work were ever we want and earn what we deserve," others seemed to hope for an alternative future where choice enters into the field of work: "justice and freedom means that you can do what you please and you can work for who you please. It means to be free. it is when you don't have to work for people and you have the right to do what you want." Another points to the power of "the head dudes" who "say what you do, when you do it and the consequences of your actions. If he says you did something, then you did and you can't do anything about it."

In another posting, two Latino students, writing together and addressing an African American student, communicate their dissent and solidarity: "Life is like bag chettoes immingratien always out to get you for something you did not do. duke you know how police is after you, well immigration is always after [us] too." The writers' analogy is enigmatic but might be taken to mean, "Life is like a bag of Cheetoes. Unlike a box of chocolates, you always know what you're going to get." When a white male student posts that freedom is guaranteed to everyone, unless a person breaks the law, a Latino student responds, "I disagree on the freedom should be taken away because i know how it felt when immigration kicked me back to Mexico in 1987 [1997?]." A Latino student picks up on a passing mention in a white female's posting about the importance of not being judged for skin color, amplifying on that submerged point by asking, "But how would you stop racist crime and punish those who have committed them?" Her reply: "I'm not sure." While a few maintained that there was no justice for the accused, one student raised the point that the victim is the one who does not receive justice, citing as an example the murder of a family member where the killer was never brought to justice. Others pressed the point that justice is subverted by those with more money and influence: "Justice is that when you're right you don't get screwed over by someone who has more money or more influence than you do. When you do something bad you get punished, fairly."

The sharpness implied in that critique, however, here and many other times, gets flattened into terms of good versus bad, individual merit versus demerit, losing the racial edge crucial to critical engagement of the larger social, systemic issues involved in the meting out of justice: "I think that this play says that freedom is a commodity that good people can rarely afford. It can be twisted and used for the benefit of jerks and idiots. The only way you can gain the proper justice is by being influntial or a bloody liar." That posting drew five responses all affirming the principle of being in the wrong place at the wrong time. The potential critical engagement thus becomes further degraded from merit to just bad luck, human agency lost altogether.

The issue of systemic injustice did keep resurfacing, but usually without direct response from anyone, much less the kind of sustained discussion so necessary to critical engagement. No one responded to the Latina female student's declaration that she would fight for keeping the dams un-breached; nor did anyone respond to the Tribal School students' assertions. This is just one example of a provocative posting that went unanswered:

> In today many people beilive that the police is a hunter ready to kill any minority that come up with minor crimes. Take the case of Rodeny King the police nearly killed him with those nightsticks. [A Latino male in the class] once was chased by police dogs because he though they were giving aways free samples at Best Buy.

THE TYRANNY OF THE MAJORITY

Why did provocative comments such as these so often go unremarked? Put another way, what factors negatively affected critical engagement in these discussions?

The most obvious factor is lack of adequate access, both at school and at home. That last-cited posting mentioning the Rodney King beating, for example, was posted on the last day of the project during the last 10 minutes of that class period. It is doubtful that anyone ever read it. With access limited to the school, and further constrained by the class period, thoughtful postings are far less likely. While some of the students did have Internet-connected computers at home, I am told, they were generally not allowed to use them. Homework is problematic in working-class families, because students often work after school and because the home is the site of family life, not schoolwork. Further, the technical upkeep of equipment adds time and money to the cost of home access, a situation that is exacerbated in large families, where allowing all children time on the computer would surely add to parental frustrations at the end of a working day. In light of this context, it is amazing to see that the Garland students read each other's postings and wrote consistently thoughtful ideas.

Tribal School students responded and were responded to far less frequently because their access was even more limited. The central server for the school was down for about a month during the project, so students composed their messages and copied them to the teacher's diskette, who then posted her students' comments at her own home computer at night. Even when the server was up, students had limited access to computers, often going to other classrooms to use the computers in those rooms to post messages. Thus Tribal School students rarely had the opportunity to read, much less follow, the discussion. Given the contexts in both schools, the students' comments seem actually more reflective and astute than one would expect.

Another factor adversely affecting critical engagement is the interplay between proximity and distance and norms of politeness. Previous scholarship on linguistic behavior in online environments focuses either on distant partners who have never met or on college students in hybrid classes, who meet each other for the first time in college. In high school classes, students often have a long history of affiliation. Whether friends or foes in the social hierarchy of high school culture, students are "family." Familiarity may breed contempt, but more often it just breeds frankness. When interacting with distant partners that they have never met, however, high school students follow their community's norms for politeness with strangers. And when those partners are proximally distant—close geographically but distant politically and culturally—those norms may be even more rigidly followed. The Garland–Tribal School electronic record strongly suggests that Garland students seemed disinclined to disagree with the Tribal School students, while the Tribal School students consistently challenged the Garland students. And both Garland and Tribal School students were more confrontational among themselves than with students from the other school.

But the most debilitating factor affecting critical engagement is what James Madison in *The Federalist Papers* called "the tyranny of the majority." Madison predicted that democracy would be imperiled if a self-interested majority failed to rule fairly for all—if, for example, 51% did not represent the views and interests of 100%. If such a majority pursued their own self-interests, in effect 51% would have 100% of the power, and 49% would become disenfranchised and disengaged. Madison warned that "the tyranny of the majority" required safeguards to protect the very notion of a participatory democracy. The concept was popularized by Lani Guinier, President Clinton's first nominee for assistant attorney general for civil rights before he withdrew her nomination in 1993. By way of illustrating one possible safeguard, Lani Guinier offered this story: She and her 4-year-old son Nicholas were reading a problem-solving story in a Sesame Street magazine about six children trying to decide which game to play.

Four wanted to play tag; two wanted to play hide-and-seek. Which game do the children play? Nicholas's answer was that they should first play tag, and then they should play hide-and-seek. His answer, Guinier explains, illustrates a "positive sum solution" (Media Education Foundation, 1995). The "winners" are awarded the privilege of going first, but the wishes of the "losers" are not entirely disregarded. A winner-takes-all, competitive style of decision making works from a zero-sum notion of power; whereas a taking-turns model understands democracy as a collaboration of multiple, often conflicting, perspectives. Those perspectives are important in finding creative solutions that go beyond "I win/you lose" (Guinier, 1998; Media Education Foundation, 1995).

That the Garland students intuitively understood the tyranny of the majority is evident in several postings, as this one illustrates: "i would fight as far as to going to the supreme court . . . if i don't have anyone not a single person behind me, i would give up becuase i would think it would be for the best." The sheer number of postings, over 1,200 in all in this particular project, among which only a small percentage represented voices of dissent, tends to enact a tyranny of a majority. Plurality of opinion stands in for consensus without weighing in all sides of an issue. Ironically, the strength of online discussions is also their weakness: While they are democratic, they are not necessarily egalitarian. Everyone can speak, but not everyone is heard. Indeed, on occasion, the Garland teacher posted messages to the discussion in an attempt to get students to dig deeper and to make connections to modern politics, but hers like other voices were simply drowned out by the cacophony of voices, where the number of similar responses tends to count as the winning opinion.

IMPLICATIONS FOR TEACHING

I maintain that online discussions within classes and between schools can be a powerful tool for critical engagement. Further, I would argue that one cannot practice a critical pedagogy in the electronic age *without* using two-way communication technologies, such as e-mail, Listservs, and online threaded discussions. But how can teachers overcome these potentially debilitating factors?

First, we need to always bear in mind that the venues of class discussion—in class or online—are complementary rather than competing pedagogies. The centrifugal force of the online discussion, which accounts for its openness and near 100% participation rate, can be re-centered and focused by the centripetal force of in-class, whole-class discussion. Before taking students online, teachers need to make explicit the goals of critical pedagogy generally and of the unit under discussion specifically. Written discussion prompts in the online environment itself, as was done in this project, ask them questions that matter to their lives. The teacher thereby validates the importance of their opinion for constructing new understandings of the material. Such practices provide a solid social and intellectual framework for critical engagement.

Organizing the online discussion in small groups, as was done in this project, proves crucial not only for limiting the amount of information coming at readers on screen but also for giving all participants a better chance to be read. A time lag between initial posting and subsequent responses also encourages critical reflection, which can be further enhanced when students are reminded to take into account ideas that came up during the intervening in-class discussions. This kind of back-and-forth, this kind of pacing, this kind of small-group structuring are all-important considerations in creating an optimal opportunity for students to actually practice participatory democracy.

But most important of all are the activities and class management structures that follow in the classroom after online discussion, for these activities and structures can enable a power distribution that enacts an egalitarian, turn-taking democracy where all views are not only expressed and read online but also one where all views are heard and considered in class. Follow-up activities have received far less attention in the scholarship on computer-mediated instruction, and then largely in regard to single classes at the college level (see e.g., Gruber, 1995; Warschauer, 1999; Warshauer, 1995). In projects such as this one, where several large classes are participating at infrequent intervals because of limited access, follow-up discussion needs to be especially structured to insure more egalitarian participation.

The same small-group discussions online can be the vehicle for managing the discussion in class afterwards in any number of ways. In any case, the online discussion, or portions thereof, needs to be brought back into the face-to-face classroom. For example, the teacher, or a student facilitator, might focus on one group's discussion each week as the springboard for whole-class discussion. Or the small groups might reconvene in class and collaborate on writing a one-page position paper that represents all views in their respective groups. Minority views are represented in proportion perhaps but never excluded altogether. These position papers might then be read to the class, perhaps just focusing on one group's position paper per week.

In sum, all or some of the transcripts of the small-group discussions need to be analyzed and synthesized, ideally by student facilitators, not (just) the teacher. And they need to be analyzed and synthesized, not according to majority rule but by rule of all-inclusiveness, where minority political opinions, no matter how unpopular, have a real hearing, not just a virtual airing. Having to paraphrase oppositional views requires that students learn empathetic listening (Media Education Foundation, 1995) or "positioned listening" (Welsh, 2001, p. 570) where the listener holds a very different subject position but can understand why people from other subject positions might hold oppositional views. Just how much emphasis to give minority views is one that students will need to decide, as they experiment with different ways of organizing "democracy," as they practice different ways to build consensus and work toward creative solutions that go beyond dichotomous, winner-take-all thinking.

Such framing and following activities complement each other, especially when the class is working on inquiry-based, thematic units, for such activities work recursively as the class grows as a learning community to arrive at deeper understandings that would not occur to them individually otherwise. Such a classroom becomes a laboratory for social justice—a crucible for proportionate democracy—where the majority does not automatically rule, where the enduring lesson is that "democracy—like learning—is often social, interactive, cooperative, and ongoing, as opposed to individualistic, isolated, competitive, and static" (Guinier, 1998, p. 309). These principles integrate the virtues of both venues, online and in-class, to create a critical pedagogy for the electronic age.

Without online threaded discussions within classes and between schools, our repertoire of critical teaching tools is simply incomplete. This particular project offers demonstration that enough students in a multiracial classroom are aware at some level of the contradictions between their lived experience and the idealized myth of America to spur the class to reflect more critically. Other schools with different kinds of populations, such as Tribal School in this project, might serve to introduce alternative perspectives. Those perspectives become more important with decreasing distance—not greater, as is the case with many long-distance "key-pal" projects—when the schools involved online have different but real political stakes in the conversation because the issues are local. The greater the distance between schools, the more likely they are to perceive the other as exotic, and the interaction becomes less threatening politically. Topics of local politics become more taboo with proximity because they are potentially more inflammatory, as was clearly the case with the Garland–Tribal School project.

Obviously, the interaction between the two schools, which was minimal because of the paucity of access, did not lead to a discussion of their respective communities' positions on breaching the dams or the tribal termination movement or any other local issues roiling in the region. If it had, very likely it would have been the same polarized discussion that dominates the public debate, without any new insights for creating new solutions. But with sustained contact, that kind of discussion might take place, and with practice and familiarity, it might take place more productively.

In the meantime, projects such as this one gives students an opportunity to learn to listen and to practice turn-taking democracy, where new solutions evolve when participants break out of either-or, pro-con arguments. Different groups have different political agendas relative to their economic status, their cultures, their group histories, as well as their personal histories and aspirations, largely defined by popular, mainstream culture, by family and tribal affiliations, by religious values, or any combination of these informing influences among others. This is a lesson that all students need. Because subjectivity is never unitary and static, consciousness may be contradictory even as it is critical. Some want to buy new boots; others want to keep old moccasins. But even as those different orientations in the world yield very different ambitions for the future, all children's schooling nonetheless should have a common goal: a critical literacy preparatory to creating a more inclusive society. Online threaded discussion is one method that promotes that kind of literacy education.

The Garland–Tribal School project also teaches us how little we actually know about computer-mediated instruction in high school classrooms comprised of underserved cultural groups. In college classrooms, the research shows, power hierarchies online tend to reconstitute along the same race, class, and gender lines as those in the traditional classroom, with the more articulate students, whose linguistic adeptness required in the academy matches the verbal behavior of the ruling elite, dominate online discussions as well, especially in the physical absence of a professor to control whose views are weighted and whose are not (W. Butler, 1992). Linguistic domination, however, was not evident in the same way in the Garland–Tribal School transcript. While some students certainly wrote more and some certainly were responded to more than others, those dominations did not follow traditional hierarchies, most probably because these high school classrooms were not constituted along the traditional hierarchies of race, class, and gender found in college classrooms, especially those where whiteness and wealth predominate. Instead, other values seemed in force, for example, working-class and cultural values and verbal behaviors very different from those valued in the elite college classroom—values such as speaking up, openly disagreeing, sharing personal experience, and taking risks, at the same time doing so in good faith and with general good will.

"Educators need to know what happens in the world of the children with whom they work. They need to know the universe of their dreams, the language with which they skillfully defend themselves from the aggressiveness of their world, what they know independently of the school and how they know it" (Freire, 1998, p. 72). The language with which students "skillfully defend themselves from the aggressiveness of their world" recorded in online environments give educators and researchers alike a window on classrooms in disenfranchised communities, an opportunity still too rare, in part because of the lack of access, to be sure, but also because of a failure to understand and fully appreciate the institutional constraints and the ideology of schooling in high-poverty schools especially, where students are tracked for low-skilled or no-skills jobs.

Getting students' words and their parallel worlds out in the public domain and then engaging others similarly oppressed via interschool online discussion—this is but one example of a pedagogy that can kindle critical consciousness. At these moments when teachers and students gain at least minimal insight into the complex forces that forge their lives and livelihoods, literacy becomes more than an educational enterprise. It becomes a political act.

CHAPTER 4

Storytime on the Reservation

In a town park in the Pacific Northwest stands a bronze sculpture of two children, each reading a book. Sitting back-to-back, they support one another like bookends. The female child is older than the male child, a fact suggesting that they are siblings rather than friends. The large-format books in their laps are about an inch thick, the typical dimensions of children's literature read in the early grades of elementary school. The sculpture is entitled "Storytime."

This piece of public art says much about mainstream values regarding the importance of reading early in life. The bronze children have the literacy skills to read for themselves, without assistance from parents or teachers. They are solitary, silent readers, but sitting in a public place where their private acts of reading are on display. Less obviously on display is the implicit message that the bronze children come from a "good" home, where their parents must have instilled in them a love of reading long before they learned to read independently and at their leisure. As implied by the name of the sculpture, "storytime" laid the foundation for their reading habits today and forever. During storytime, their parents taught them the literacy skills to decode words and pictures on a page; moreover, they also socialized them to use language and to learn in certain ways, using the story and illustrations as mere touch points for their conversation. It was this dyadic interaction between parent and child, not the story per se, that expanded their sense of literateness (Heath, 1984). Through talk about stories, the parents imparted to their children not only a sense of literateness, but also an epistemology.

As if it were also cast in bronze, that epistemology is assumed to be universal and natural, at least for "normal" children with "good" parents. To be sure, thousands of studies have confirmed the importance of bedtime story reading in preparing children for school success (Wolf & Heath,

85

1992).[1] Most of these studies have centered on white, middle-class children, and most often on very young children, before preschool, or children in the early grades of elementary school. Much less is known about the language socialization practices in the homes of low-income children of color, and even less about the impact of those practices on their academic performance in secondary school (Heath, 1991; Wolf & Heath, 1992).

In short, many kinds of distances—geographic, social, racial—have foreshortened previous understandings of the impact of cultural differences on language use and learning. But now that rural schools are coming online, and with the advent of Web-based e-mail, another channel of communication has opened up, one that has the potential for connecting rural, low-income communities of color with predominately white universities. Unfortunately, although high-poverty schools are online, their students are not, for reasons I will broach at the end of this chapter. But their teachers *are* online, especially at home where they also have time to converse, and teacher-to-professor interaction via e-mail can help establish the trust prerequisite for partnership between universities and distant schools where other cultural majorities prevail. And when these schools connect with teacher preparation programs—as opposed to writing centers, as was the case in Chapter 2—the interinstitutional relationship can be significantly revised: Instead of writing centers helping schools, schools can help English teacher preparation programs better understand the cultural contingencies of the writing and rhetoric of nonwhite students.

These were precisely the conditions that made possible the fieldwork that served as the primary material for this chapter. Under examination here is a school year's worth of writing by 50 seventh-grade students from a remote public school on a Plateau Indian reservation (I leave the tribe unspecified to protect the anonymity of the school). Their teacher collected approximately 800 papers over the course of the 2001–02 school year and sent them via postal mail to me as the English education coordinator at a university several hours away. In turn, I use some of this material with the preservice teachers in my methods course on teaching writing. More importantly, this collection offers for the first time a comprehensive view of the contrasting discursive practices of Latino, Plateau Indian, white, and Filipino students—and at an age least examined in educational research: the edge of adolescence.

Based on students' own reports on household routines in several different assignments, coupled with the contrastive rhetoric evident in their writing, this ethnographic and discursive analysis offers fresh insights into the cultural differences in language socialization in nonwhite homes. These students' lives and literacies are saturated in electronic media of all kinds—video games, e-mail, and chat—but most strikingly, television. What is conspicuously absent in these self-reports on home life is the ritual of bed-time story reading; in its stead is TV watching.[2] I ultimately maintain that electronic media—mainly, movies and e-mail—can bridge the gaping maw between home and school literacies of Latino and American Indian students in particular.[3]

In this multiracial community, storytime holds cultural content quite foreign to mainstream ways; at the same time, storytime in the electronic age is mainly delivered through movies, the common culture of teenagers, regardless of ethnicity. Thus movies can be used productively in reservation schools to teach critical literacy, and e-mail and other forms of online discussion hold promise for nonwhite students who learn best from peer demonstration. This kind of curriculum and pedagogy would make explicit that mainstream epistemology is an acquired way, not a natural way, of looking at the world. In short, for working-class students of color, academic literacy might be best understood as interethnic communications, and popular culture and computer-mediated discussion might provide the best ways for these students to make that crossover.

LOCAL CONTEXTS

Home to approximately a thousand families, the town of Rondo (a pseudonym) is located on one of the largest Indian reservations in the region.[4] Although Rondo is just off an interstate highway, with small cities within a half hour's drive, it feels isolated, sitting as it does amid flat fields and ranch lands in Indian country. The town center has the windswept look of many impoverished rural towns, its railroad tracks and abandoned warehouses falsely evoking a more prosperous past. Unlike rural towns in other parts of the country, however, this one is distinctly multiracial, its diversity reflecting local history and economics. The Dawes Act of 1887 opened up reservation lands to non-Indian settlement. Although most of the settlers a hundred years ago were white Euro-Americans, immigrants later trekked from Mexico and, to a much lesser extent but most recently, from the Philippines. The lure of agricultural jobs drew them to the region, and low wages have kept them there. A large and stable Latino community also provides support networks for those who follow. That so many Latinos of Mexican descent call this region home has somehow bypassed national consciousness.

Although Rondo sits in the migration stream in this agricultural region, its population has not fluctuated much over the past decade, at least not in numbers, newcomers apparently replacing residents who move on to nearby towns. About 33% of the population are foreign born; an overwhelming majority (90%) of this group come from Mexico. Most recently, Rondo has seen an influx of Filipino immigrants, who make up about 1.2% of the population. Other figures suggest that most residents here are first- and second-generation immigrants. Spanish is spoken in about 66% of the homes, Filipino-Tagalog in about 4%, and English only in just 30%. The Plateau Indian language group accounts for the only other languages spoken at home, in conjunction with either English or Spanish.

Ethnic groups here coexist, with little tension between groups, but possibly because the community's caste-like hierarchy has become naturalized. Everyone knows everyone because everyone is related, teachers have told me, but demographic statistics suggest that ethnic groups tend to stay with their own. Of all residents of only one race-ethnicity, 25% are white, 0.5% are African American, 9.3% are American Indian (the U.S. Census leaves tribes unspecified), and 1.2% are Filipino. Of all residents with mixed heritage, the percentages of American Indian and Filipino are slightly higher (10.8% and 2.4%, respectively), and the percentage for African Americans is slightly lower (0.09%). Anywhere from 61% to 69% of the town is Latino of Mexican descent, either solely or in combination with another ethnic group.

Rondo's diversity also speaks to the abiding segregation of immigrant and Plateau Indian groups, relegated to pockets of poverty on a vast reservation, apart from mainstream ways and means. Rondo is one such pocket. The community maintains a stable, if subsistent economy, with agriculture and the local school district as the main sources of jobs. The median earnings for males working full-time, year round is $18,333; for females, $19,375. About 55% of the homes in Rondo are owner-occupied, with 45% renter-occupied—a relatively high rental rate marking the community as low-income, low–inherited wealth, and high–physical mobility. The unemployment rate is 13%—a rate substantially better than the 90% unemployment rate on the reservation generally. Even though Rondo is prosperous by reservation standards, poverty is as abiding as skin color. About 32% of all families in Rondo live in poverty; 55% of all families headed up by females without husbands present live in poverty. Families are variously configured: Extended families commonly live under the same roof, and about 46% of all grandparents are primary caregivers for their grandchildren.

In the one middle school that serves this community, two seventh-grade classes participated in the research project under discussion in this chapter. The demographics of those two classes differed slightly from those of the town generally, the representation by ethnicity more evenly distributed.[5] Of the 49 students in the project, most were only one ethnicity: 23 Latinos of Mexican descent; 12 Plateau Indians; 3 whites; and 3 Filipinos.

Six students had more than one ethnic background: 1 Plateau Indian–Latino; 1 Plateau Indian–African American; 2 Plateau Indian–white; 1 Latino–white; and 1 Latino–Filipino. Two students did not identify their ethnic backgrounds. The first language of 17 students was Spanish; another 8 students said Spanish was their second language. Filipino-Tagalog was spoken in one home, and a Plateau Indian language were spoken in one other, as well as English. Academically, school scores on the state-mandated exam in reading and writing at the seventh grade are the lowest in the state.

In the course of the school year, the teacher at Rondo Middle School sent me 30 sets of papers written on 15 assignments, with another handful of papers on various make-up assignments. Six of those 15 assignments were narratives of three distinct types. One type called for strict chronologies in a certain time period: "My MLK Weekend," "A Typical Day [of a Seventh Grader]," and "Spring Break." Students also wrote two personal narratives on something that had happened to them or someone they knew. The third type of assignment asked students to create a fictional narrative based on a two-dimensional picture. An analysis of this fictional narrative assignment, coupled with information gleaned from students' other nonfictional narrative assignment, reveals much about these students' home lives and literacies. Their performance on this assignment, which was a practice prompt for the state-mandated test, is also predictive of their chances for successfully mastering academic literacy.

Before embarking on this analysis, however, I want to offer several important caveats. First, when I speak of cultural differences in storytelling, I am not essentializing culture. Not all narratives written by Latino students in Rondo share all of the discursive features that I am about to describe; in like manner, not all Plateau Indian students encoded performance cues in their stories. Still, the generalization holds true: most Latino students consistently produced discourse of reserve, while the students of other ethnicities produced elaborated discourse: White and Filipino students elaborated in distinctive ways while Plateau Indian students elaborated using other techniques, described below. Why ethnic differences in storytelling emerge in this student paper collection has nothing to do with biology and everything to do with early language socialization in the home.

Second, ethnicity alone should not be taken as having predictive value. A teacher should not prejudge that an individual student will automatically produce a certain kind of narrative, basing that prediction solely on a student's ethnicity. Insofar as language use in the home conforms to ethnic norms, so a child's literacy development will be typical for that ethnic group.

Third, teachers need to recognize that there is no "natural" way to tell a story. Storytelling, as well as more generally taking meaning from written and visual materials, is learned behavior informed by group norms, as much as table manners, interior decorating, and personal dress (Heath, 1986; see also Dyson & Genishi, 1994; Miller & Mehler, 1994). Both as a genre and as a communicative act, storytelling follows the contours of what has been defined as appropriate by a discursive community as well as by family traditions (Miller, Hoogstra, Mintz, Fung, & Williams, 1994).

And finally, the standards for judging a story's quality—such as vivifying details, dramatic dialogue, fleshed-out characters, and inventive plot lines—have become naturalized and dominate the way we judge literature as well as student narratives, both fictional and nonfictional. Unfortunately, these Euro-centric standards have been taken for granted as universal by state-test scorers, if not most teachers. Other ways of telling a story and judging its quality get subsumed by those valued by white culture, just as the norms for academic literate behavior more generally also get defined by white norms.

With these caveats in mind, the discussion at hand will provide a productive starting point for understanding exactly how and why certain ethnic groups have such great difficulty with academic literacy. How teachers should address this difficulty will be explored at the end of this chapter.

WRITING A FICTIONAL NARRATIVE

Toward the end of the school year, and after students had written two personal narratives, the teacher gave students a prompt called "The Creek" (see accompanying illustration) which asks students to create a fictional narrative based on the two-dimensional drawing. The immediate purpose of the assignment was to practice for the writing portion of the state-mandated test, which is required at the fourth-, seventh-, and tenth-grade levels; students must pass the tenth-grade test before they can graduate with a high school diploma. Actually, the state writing test never asks students above the fourth-grade level to write narratives; further, the state test no longer uses two-dimensional drawing in narrative prompts for fourth graders because such drawings, it was found, limit students' thinking (Nikki Elliott-Schuman, personal communication, April 21, 2003). Still, the prompt makes sense within the curriculum sequence of these two classes. Because this was practice, and not the real exam, the teacher went over the questions in class orally and brainstormed some possibilities for each of the questions, practicing with them on how to approach a test question to ensure that all parts are individually addressed.

To score well, writers would need to identify what the girl sees in the water, the more detail, the better: for example, not just a fish, but a trout;

Day One: Writing Assessment

Directions: Today you will write a story based on the picture below. Take a moment to look at the picture.

The Creek

Write a story based on this picture.

An effective writer may consider the following points:
- Who are these young people?
- Do they live near the creek, or are they visitors?
- What were they doing before they started crossing the creek?
- What has the girl noticed in the water?
- Why is she signalling for her friend to be quiet?
- What will happen next?

not just a trout, but a rainbow trout; not just a frog, but a bullfrog; not just a bullfrog, but a huge bullfrog that goes "ribbit." Writers would need to predict what happens after the series of questions listed in the prompt, which are only intended as exposition fillers. Vivifying detail, such as description of the characters' physical and emotional states, and dialogue that fleshes out characterization and advances plot will also raise scores.

Latino Students' Narratives

What were the prevailing discursive features of narratives produced by the Latino students? Most answered the questions listed with the prompt in literal, nonelaborated ways. Almost all of the students give the two characters names—which the teacher suggested that they do—although they rarely identify the characters' relationship as siblings, relatives, or friends. The trajectory of the plot implied in the prompt is largely followed, with the answer to the last question—"What will happen next?"—concluding, rather than complicating, the plot line. Only a few writers had their characters leave the setting depicted in the picture. Few of the stories have dialogue, and then conversation is largely reported in indirect quotation rather than recorded as direct quotation. There is little variation in what the two characters see: Most often, the girl sees a fish or a frog and calls the boy over. In some of the narratives, the two characters decide to capture the creature and take it to their guardians, who usually counsel that the boy and girl return the creature to its natural habitat. But most often, the creature is simply observed and eventually swims away, untouched and unharmed by the two characters, who then also depart. In a few instances, the writer continues the report of the characters' day with other wildlife sightings. The following is fairly representative of Latino students' narratives about The Creek:

> These young people are a boy and a girl and these young people are just visiting the creek. What they are doing is they were eating lunch then they decided to look at the creek. Then the girl noticed a fish in the creek Jumping in the water because she didn't want to scar[e] the fish she told her friend to be quiet. She took a closer look at the fish to see what color it was.[6]

This same reportage style is evident in the following piece written by John (a pseudonym) as well, but this one is unusual in its length and use of detail. Still, notice how tentatively John assigns motives to the characters, preferring to stick to verifiable, literal facts.

The Creek

These young people are one boy and one girl they are stepping on stones. I think they're visitors because at the left far end is a blanket and a basket on top of it so they are probably having a picnic. They were eating under a tree, I think the girl noticed fishes in the water.

The girl was singaling to her friend to be quiet and to come and see the fish in the water. I think they are going to try and catch a fish. They probably want to catch a fish so they could take it home. After they caught the fishes they got tired and went to drink something cause they were really thirsty and tired.

After they finished resting they packed their picnic and started hiking home. They got to see lots of animals on their way home. They crossed a bridge that was going over a river and stoped at some public Restrooms. They seen bugs and bald eagles. When they got home they gave the two fishes to their dad and he cleand them. The two children that went to the creek were beat of all the hiking they had to do so they took a shower and went to sleep.

The End

This example is unusual in another regard: the writer extends the story beyond the immediate depiction, predicting what the characters might do after leaving the creek.

Most Latino student writers, however, included very little vivifying detail or specificity. In the following example, the writer does include specifics, but does so at the expense of plot and relevance, as we see in this example, quoted in its entirety:

The people are visiting a state park. They from Texas There names are Jim and Sam. They are visiting the state park because it is Sam birthday. They are staying here for a couple of days they want to explore the out-doors. The state they are visiting is in Kansas. Jim said there are some pretty nice people around here.

Interestingly, the writer records, rather than reports, Jim's words, a feature generally not present in other Latino students' responses to this prompt.

Plateau Indian Students' Narratives

Dialogue, both its use and the purpose of that use, is the discursive feature that most conspicuously marks the difference between Latino and non-Latino student writing in this collection. In the following example, a Plateau Indian male student uses dialogue—idiomatic and enigmatic at the same time—to develop characterization and plot.

Looking for fish

One day there was a boy named Jeff and his sister Annia. They where out on a pitneck in the forest by there house. Annia saw the creek the creek was by there house to. Jeff packed all there stuff for the pikneck.

Jeff said we better eat are stuff in the basket. Before the ants come and try to get some food from us. Annia said okay so Annie had a sandwich and so did Jeff. Then Annia said I beat [bet] there fish in that creek. Jeff said not even theres no fish in creeks.

After Annia was done eating. She went to go see if there were fish in the creek. Jeff was still eating his sandwich. Then Annia stood on a rock and looked over and saw a fish. She quietly said Jeff come here look at this. Annia signaling to be quiet so that Jeff wouldn't scare the fish away. Then Annia's and Jeff's Mom called for them to come home.

After this happened Annia looked down and the fish was gone. All wells at least I know theres fish in the creek Annia said. Jeff says we have to go now so go get the pitneck basekt please. Allright said Annia she got the pitneck basekt and went home.

One difficulty in reading this piece is, of course, the nonstandard spelling, punctuation, sentence boundaries, and the like. That issue aside, the story's meaning hinges largely on how we read Jeff's words early in the story and the intent behind those words: "Not even theres no fish in creeks." Is he just joking around with his sister, or is he challenging her in some way? Either may be the case, since fish do inhabit creeks, although maybe not this particular one.[7] When Annia sees a fish and signals Jeff over, their mother's call apparently scares the fish away. Did Jeff see the fish before it swam away? We do not know, nor does Annia, because he does not verbally acknowledge the sighting or even her signal. Annia, however, does not need his acknowledgement after all, self-validating her own perception: "at least I know." Trusting one's own senses is the lesson that the brother Jeff leads his sister toward, even if inadvertently on the writer's part, and one that she learns not through words but experience. In like manner, the story's complex character dynamic and theme go unexplicated by the storyteller, who allows readers to experience the story for themselves, not through words.

In another story, Paul (a pseudonym), another Plateau Indian male student, begins from the first-person point of view of the female character. Both characters have names of classmates romantically linked in the class—a fact that his peers recognized and enjoyed immensely. That Paul switches point of view from first- to third-person after three sentences suggests that he is gauging how long it will take his audience to react—and for the joke to get old. His timing is impeccable. Notice that the plot is largely developed through dialogue (as it is in "Looking for Fish"), this time marked with intonation cues: shouting, stuttering, and so forth.

Hello, my name is Mary. I am here with my boyfriend Mike [drawing of a heart]. We were at home when Mary said "lets go for a picnic."

But Mike said "No, because I am waching Mens finalls track race." But Mary took no for in answer. "We are going." she said politely, AND YOU ARE COMMING Mister" She yelled. Mike's eyes were as big as his head. He got packed within 2 minutes. As they were going to the picnic they stop at the store to get some food. The ranger's house was not that far away. They only lived 1-1/2 miles away from it, so they walk. When they get ther the ranger said are you going to stay the night or just visiting? Mary said "we are just visitors. As they went to go find a place to picnic, they found a nice one under a tree right by the creek. As they were going to sit down, Mike said "I . . . . . I . . . . . I, um forgot the . . . . .

Mary interups and say "What did you forget" . . . . . . (mike still did not answer) . . . . "Well, SPEAK UP MIKE!!!!.

Mike says "I forgot the . . . . . the . . . . . . the blanket. Mary's eyes almost poped out of her head. "You WHAT" she shrieked. "We will just have to use your coat" Mary says Well lets eat . . . . (5 min.) . . . . (10 min.). "Yum, that was go—(BURP) . . . . . opps sorry," Mike says. "Come on lets go to the other side of the creek." she asked. So they both go to the rock's where they can walk on and over. Just then Mary saw something in the water. She saw a fish. She saw Mike munching away on a drumstick "MUNCH, Munch." "Shhhhh, be quit look a rianbow trout. Come one lets go Home."

By Paul Williams

Clearly Paul sees storytelling as an act of performance: his story reads like a script. Interestingly, he seems keenly aware that this performance also has a paper dimension to it, for he artfully includes a drawing of a heart and arranges his byline with visual flair. (In fact, all of his writings have both oral and written marks of performance: miniature artwork as cartoonlike illustration and visual indication of intonation.) And once again, there is the same significant subtext as in "Looking for Fish": the playful power struggle between males and females.

In both "Looking for Fish" and Paul's untitled story, another feature appears: the use of finite detail. In "Looking for Fish," Jeff cautions that ants might get into the picnic basket; Paul has his characters living 1-1/2 miles away. In another story not quoted here, a Plateau Indian female student writes that the characters see the fish in the creek because it is stuck in a plastic bag. Throughout the Rondo collection, Plateau Indian students consistently use this kind of finite detail, and often in the service of having a scene or a point make more common sense: Because of the ants, Jeff and Annia eat first; because they live relatively close by, Mary and Mike can walk to this creek.

White Students' Narratives

A different kind of detail, however, shows up in the writing of the white students in this project: vivifying detail. While "show, don't tell" is a mantra of narrative writing generally, using vivifying detail also holds syntactic implications, as greater degrees of modification become embedded within more complex sentence structures. In short, this kind of vivifying detail is key to ultimately producing elaborated discourse—the kind of discourse most valued in academic writing. Notice not only the concrete (and inventive) details but also the variety of sentence structures and lengths in the narratives produced by white students: "The Creek" and "Johnny and Jane."

The Creek

One summer afternoon the Johnsons decided to have a picnic up in the meadow in the park. They packed fried chicken, apple sauce, mashed potatoes and milk.

After they were done eating Mr. and Mrs. Johnson decided to go for a walk, but their two kids: Allen and Shirley didn't want to go with them but on a walk by themselves. They walked along the creek to try to catch some interesting things.

They didn't have to go very far, Allen almost caught a snake, but it got away. All of the sudden Shirley saw a huge bullfrog. Shirley was going to sneak up on it, so she motioned Allen to be quiet. She walked out onto some stones in the middle of the creek and was about to grab it when she lost her balance and fell in!

Right then their parents came up and helped her out of the the
water. Shirley was wet all of the way home but really didn't mind,
she had a good time just like the rest of the family!
The End

Johnny + Jane

One day Johnny and Jane decided to take a walk along the creek.
They have lived by the creek all their lives, so they know the creek
pretty well. Johnny saw some Rocks and though it would be fun to
use the Rock to cross the creek. As they were crossing Jane saw a
frog swimming in the Creek. Jane quietly said, "shh, if we be quiet
and sneaky, we could catch him." Johnny agreed. It wasn't easy. In
the doing so, Jane fell in the Water and Johnny landed on top of her,
And the worst thing is, Jane was wearing her new shirt from Macy's.
They finally did end up catching the frog. When Jane and Johnny
caught the frog, the[y] named the frog, "Carl." (Do[n]t ask me why
they named him Carl, they just did, ok) They decided to take Carl
home so they could find a good place to put him inside.

When they got home, Mama was enraged when she saw Jane's
brand new clothes from Macy's. Enoyed, Mama said, "What in
God's Green Earth have you children been doing!!!"

Johnny spoke up and said, "Well Mama, as we were walking
along the creek, Jane saw a frog, so we tried to catch it, and when
we were catching it, Jane fell in." "Ah, I see," said Mama. "Jane,
you go to your room and change your clothes and I'll wash them for
you." "Thank you" said Jane appriciatly.

After Jane finished changing her clothes, Johnny and her got a
jar, made holes in it, got some grass and put Carl in it. And Carl,
Johnny, and Jane lived happily ever after.

BEDTIME STORY AS EPISTEMOLOGY

Why did most of the Latino students produce literal and restrained accounts of what might have happened at the creek, whereas most of the
non-Latino students did not?

Differences in literate behavior—as opposed to literacy skills, which
are more narrowly focused on encoding-decoding and deriving literal
meaning—are directly attributed to how children are socialized to use language in the home. This socialization process clearly differs across socioeconomic class and ethnicity. Verbal interactions with caregivers introduce

children to distinctive sociocultural orientations in the world by initiating them into the linguistic behaviors deemed appropriate and meaningful for a particular discourse community. Learning how to talk, in the broadest sense of the phrase, entails learning certain attitudes and social roles about how to take and make meaning from the word and from the world. It also entails learning how to display that knowledge. Moreover, verbal interactions and oral and written displays of knowledge carry cultural content crucial to group and individual identity formulation and maintenance.

Of all the verbal interactions between caregivers and children, the most important to a child's developing sense of academic literateness is the ritual of the bedtime story. Notably, this literacy event is as common in white households as it is uncommon in working-class Latino homes—a point verified by the Rondo students' other autobiographical assignments describing their "Typical Day," their "MLK Weekend," and their "Spring Breaks." In short, when the ways of using language at home differ radically from the ways that language is used in school, children from those homes are going to have greater difficulty in school. Because the academic literate behavior required in school is normed on white, middle-class standards of literateness, working-class students of color too often must learn how to write, talk, and even think in ways alien to their customary ways with words if they are to achieve school success. Exactly how children from different socioeconomic class and ethnic backgrounds are acculturated to learn in certain ways is the subject now under discussion.

Socioeconomic Class Differences

Although commonplace in white households, the ritual of reading stories at bedtime nonetheless plays out differently in middle-class and working-class homes, as Heath (1986) captures in her description of parent-child interactions in fictitious Maintown and Roadville. What actually differs between the two communities is the *talk* that surrounds the bedtime story, both at the time of the literacy event and in its subsequent iterations in other verbal interactions. It is this talk about story reading—rather than the story reading itself—that establishes interactional and learning patterns that will persist through school. The degree to which those patterns are consistent with the embedded discursive forms of schooling positively predict a child's chances for academic success.

In Maintown, the ritual of the bedtime story reading gives a parent and child a regularly scheduled time to verbally interact. In the early stage of this ritual, up until the child is about 3 years old, the parent and child engage in turn-taking dialogue. The parent calls attention to two-dimensional representations in the book, labeling items and asking, "What's that?" The child answers verbally, and the parent reinforces the child's response. The parent also sequences questions, scaffolding from "what" questions to more abstract, analogic "why" questions and affective commentary. The what-questions break down content into smaller pieces, decontextualizing them for isolated consideration, explanation, classification, and categorization. While the answers to what-questions are predictable, the answers to why-questions are not. These answers require reconfiguration and recontextualization, a cognitive behavior that Maintown parents also model outside the ritual of the bedtime story, offering running commentary with the child's environment and experience, linking old with new knowledge, connecting two-dimensional representations with their counterparts in the real world. After about age 3, however, this turn taking and scaffolding dialogue is replaced with directives to sit quietly and listen until the parent signals that it is time for questions. In preschool, the child learns anew to sit quietly and await the time for response, but now she must also learn how to get attention over others who are also seeking turns to speak.

Consistently, then, from bedtime story through school in Maintown, the individual is the focus of the display of knowledge. The interactive pattern between adults and children in early childhood is the same that dominates classroom discourse: initiation-reply-evaluation. That is, the teacher asks a question that he already knows the answer to; a student responds; the teacher evaluates that response (Heath, 1986; see also Mehan, 1979; Sinclair & Coulthard, 1975). Further, what-questions with their predictable answers that can be graded right or wrong are the kind of questions that appear on standardized tests; in classroom practice, the what-questions must be answered before advancing to the why-questions, which are usually saved for enrichment. By elementary school, Maintown children have learned and have come to expect that the written word might represent not only real events but "decontextualized logical propositions" (Heath, 1986, p. 120). And they have learned that these propositions often take priority over the real, which only comes into play after what-questions have been examined (Heath, 1986). In sum, for Maintown children, the bedtime story represents the beginning of a chain of events that acculturate them to the bedrock discursive practices of school literateness and interaction.

In Roadville, a white, working-class, religious community also described by Heath (1986), bedtime story reading also offers parents and children a special time to interact. Like the Maintown version of this literacy event, Roadville children are coached to approach written and visual content with what-questions that present information in discrete bits and pieces, and parents prescribed much the same listening and knowledge-displaying behaviors. But unlike their Maintown counterparts, Roadville children are not encouraged to recontextualize and connect two-dimensional representation of information to real-life counterparts. The frame of reference does not move outside the book; stylization of pictoral representations—yellow ducks, flat balls, talking dogs—are accepted at face value. Parents do not allude to books in the child's environment, drawing parallels to something that they read the night before. The word and the world are distinct realms that do not overlap, and print simply does not carry the same authority in the world as experiential knowledge. When teaching their children generally, parents in this community might demonstrate a task to be learned, but without verbally segmenting the steps in completing the task. When a child attempts to perform that task, the parent will evaluate but without verbally reinforcing the steps or offering reasons behind the instructions.

For example, a parent might say, "That's right. Don't twist the [cookie] cutter" instead of saying, "That's right. If you twist the [cookie] cutter, the cookies will be rough on the edge" (Heath, 1986, p. 62). Further, Roadville parents generally reject shifting frames of reference or otherwise fictionalizing versions of real events—for example, bible stories told in modern settings. They hold that fictionalized narratives are "lies" (Heath, 1986, p. 111). Stories must be true to events, and they must be told by designated storytellers about people present. Stories must also have morals that represent certain truths and values that the community holds dear; therefore, events in stories are not questioned as long as they fit the community's view of the world. Embellishment or personal affective response in storytelling is relatively unheard of.

These are the cognitive and literate behaviors that Roadville children bring to their school experience. In school, when teachers ask them what they think of an ending or to come up with another one, children are generally unable to respond. When asked to write a creative story, they usually retell stories they have heard or read but rarely offer affective commentary. By fourth grade, after initial success in the earlier grades, these children begin to fall behind academically (Heath, 1986). The early and persistent emphases on following directions without why-questions, on literal interpretation of words and pictures, and on the separation between word and world have ill-prepared Roadville children for school success.

Ethnic Differences

As we see from Heath's ethnographic descriptions of Maintown and Roadville, socioeconomic class differences clearly define how children are socialized to talk—indeed, to think—in these two white communities, even though the key literacy event in both towns is the bedtime story. But bedtime story reading is largely absent in Latino families of Mexican descent. Parent-child interaction is grounded in very different premises about social roles, which are largely based on gender and age. Further, ways of deriving and displaying meaning from books and pictures differ greatly from those that characterize Maintown ways, although they bear a certain resemblance to those that characterize Roadville ways. This similarity between Roadville and Latino homes suggests that class exerts a definite influence—although not a determining influence, I argue here—on literate behavior.

Although voluntary immigrants generally lose their native tongue within two generations, their communicative styles prevail much longer (Tannen, 1981), in large part because language socialization of children remains relatively constant. In many Mexican-origin homes children are taught that they must observe and listen. They are to speak when asked direct questions, but they are not to initiate conversation. Adults do not ask questions for which they already know the answers unless they are teasing. Children are rarely alone without adult supervision. Talk in the home and a family gathering—a common affair—is segregated by gender and often by age. Unlike their white counterparts, children are not asked to recount narratives if parents also participated in the events, and they are not encouraged to perform as individual actors, especially in the presence of adults. (Heath, 1989; see also Delgado-Gaitan, 1990; Heath, 1986, 1991). In one case study on parent interaction with preschool children in daily routines, most of the talk was parent directives to the child, many of them requiring only a yes or no answer; "interactions of less than 1 minute accounted for 95.1%" of all the verbal exchanges between parent and child (Heath, 1989, p. 344). Thus the literate behaviors required in school run exactly counter to those experienced and valued in most Mexican-origin homes, as Heath (1989) sums up:

> Competitive display of knowledge by individuals [required in school] . . . breaks the social bonds and acceptance of differential levels of talent upon which many of these societies have depended for centuries. The focus on generalized knowledge across individuals, discourse forms that highlight the scope and sequence of task segments, and attention on the individual as sole actor or agent undermines the ideology and ethos of [Mexican-origin] groups. (p. 347)

TV TIME AS STORYTIME

In Mexican-origin homes, then, parent-child dyadic conversation is not normative, largely because children are not recognized as appropriate conversational partners for adults. Dyadic interaction, too, may be less common because of larger family size and smaller home size, both of which affect domestic use of space and time. Not surprisingly, the bedtime story ritual, with its emphasis on dyadic conversation, decontextualization, and individual knowledge display, at a set time of the day, is also far less common, if not nonexistent, in these households than in white households.

The Rondo paper collection unequivocally confirms that conclusion. We get descriptions on students' home life from several angles in five assignments: "All About Me," "MLK Weekend," "Spring Break," "A Typical Day," and "New Year's Resolution." In Rondo, bedtime itself is framed in much the same way as it is in Maintown and Roadville, at least on school nights: Children go to bed at a certain time, following certain routines before turning in. One consistent element of that bedtime routine is watching television. Further, the entertainment industry has generated its own genres, including reviews, blurbs, and the like, and Rondo students demonstrate in different degrees a working knowledge of these genres. In short, TV watching in Rondo is roughly equivalent to story reading in Maintown and Roadville. As such, TV and movies might serve as a bridge between home and school literateness. Not only could movie "stories" encourage students to make new linkages between different kinds of texts and their world, so could instructional uses of other electronic media, especially e-mail, chat, and threaded discussions, open up new possibilities for interacting with others and for displaying knowledge in public venues in more culturally relevant ways, as I contend in this section.

According to the questionnaires they filled out as part of this research project, students reported watching an average of 12 hours of television a week, versus 4 hours of reading for pleasure in English.[8] In describing their daily routines in "A Typical Day," only three students mention reading 30 minutes every day, and another one mentions reading an unspecified amount of time before bedtime. In their "All About Me" autobiographical descriptions, only two students mentioned having favorite books—more precisely, a book series and an author: *Goosebumps* and Shel Silverstein. Only two students (including the one who liked Silverstein) mentioned reading as a favorite pastime. Oddly enough, despite all this time devoted to watching television, students rarely mention specific television programs, although they frequently mention specific movies. Over the course of these five writing assignments, these TV programs—most of them on cable— were referenced: *Battle Bots*, *Mujer*, *La Vida*, *SpongeBob SquarePants*, *Boy Meets World*, *Sister Sister*, *One World*, and *Unsolved Mysteries*. Some mention genres of TV programs they watch, such as cartoons in the mornings and "novellas" at night. Much more commonly, students bring up movies; they name 49 titles specifically. Certain genres predominated: comedies, romantic comedies, action, and horror films.[9] Interestingly, the list includes many R-rated movies, including *American Pie II*, *Blade 2*, *Shaft*, *Road Trip*, *Scary Movie 2*, *Spring Break*, *Halloween: H20*, *Road Dogz*, and *Panic Room*.

Despite the centrality of TV in their lives, they have nonetheless adopted the general devaluation of television in this particular context, school. In their "New Year's Resolution" writing assignment, many students wrote that they needed to cut down on their TV watching and do more exercising, eat less junk food, do their homework, and make good grades. Clearly, they feel guilty about watching television or, more accurately, they think they *should* feel guilty about watching television. This devaluation of TV watching, especially when compared to book reading, is a distinctly white, middle-class attitude, and one that largely serves the status quo (Buckingham, 1993; Dyson, 1993, 1997).

Generally, movie watching is more highly valued by the white middle-class than TV watching for a couple of reasons. The length, the narrative complexity, and closure of movies have a closer relationship to novels than do TV dramas and situation comedies that work from the same premise, week-to-week; too, movie screenplays are sometimes based on novels, whereas regular programming on TV rarely is. Like reading certain kinds of books, watching certain genres of movies (e.g., Hollywood classics or dramatic films as opposed to "chick flicks") carry more social status at least in white middle-class communities. What "the reviews" say and how those reports are valued are also class-marked. Even the most casual mention of "the reviews" of a movie telegraphs that the speaker reads and has taste, and once again, the link with reading tends to legitimate one's own movie watching as a more intellectual, less passive, and therefore more worthy pastime pursuit than simply watching movies indiscriminately and without reading the critics.

The Rondo students have not internalized all of these attitudes, of course. Nonetheless, the entertainment industry generates many print genres besides full-length movie reviews, and these clearly have had their impact on the literacies of the Rondo seventh graders. These genres potentially constitute the most important source of reading materials outside of school (see also Anderson & Stokes, 1984). Genres from the entertainment domain employ different rhetorics of information that require complex literate behavior at times. A classic example is a television schedule, a table of information that uses words, numbers, colors, and shapes (to indicate different channels) must be read both horizontally as well as vertically. Another genre is the plot summary and cursory evaluation of a movie—often with quotations from critics reduced to adjectives or short phrases—in movie "trailers," on video packaging, and in summary preces in cable and satellite TV bulletins and on-screen information panels. The impact of this particular genre—and the centrality of movies on the lives of many of these students—is especially evident in the Rondo papers. In his "A Typical Day" paper, quoted in its entirety below, John, a Latino male student, writes about what he did on one specific day (rather than one typical day) in his life. Notice that over half of the paper is made up of movie synopses, not unlike the ones that might be found in movie schedules, trailers, or video boxes:

> My typical day was when I woke up on January the 27th 2002 and played Nintendo 64 until ten-thirty in the morning. When I finished playing Nintendo I got dressed and went to my friend's house and played with his little brother and her. I left at twelve twenty-five and went to my house and made a fire, I stayed making fire until three forty-five and went inside to take a shower and change.
>
> I went to the phone to call Palermo Pizza to order a large pepperoni pizza and a 2 liter pop. I told the person we were going to pick it up our order. When I got of the phone, I asked my mom if she could take me to Tio Dave's Video's to rent a couple of movies. When we got to Tio Dave's Videos I went in and looked at the movies and I looked all over to see which movie I wanted I got two movies and my brother got two movies to.
>
> I got *Baby Boy* it's about an adult who act's like a baby and gets beat up and get's his revenge. My brother got 007 *Tomorrow never dies*. This movie is about a secret agent who steal's a red box from some enemies so he could solve who boomed the German boat. I found another movie that I like it is call *The fast and the furiouse*. It's about racer's who bet money to see who wins. The called a person Snowman because he's white. He wanted to be in the race to but he didn't have cash so he bet his car. Bad news for him, he lost his car. The last movie my brother got was *Jurassic Park three*. It's about dinosaurs who could communicate with other dinosaurs that are the same type. They call for help when they need it and when the find a dinosaure to kill and eat. Afer I finished watching the movies I went to sleep at one thirty of the morning. That was my typicall day and night.

John's movie synopses of *Baby Boy* and *Tomorrow Never Dies* nicely nutshell the major plot lines of those two movies. His preces of the other two movies are not as neat. For *The Fast and Furious*, he interjects an aside about how the character Snowman got that nickname; and for *Jurassic Part III*, he only sets up a background premise propelling the plot. It should be noted, however, that this is the same John who was so tentative in offering affective commentary in his narrative based on "The Creek," which I cited earlier. Although John is still very literal in these last two preces, he is much less tentative. He shares facts about the two films that are apparently interesting to him; at the same time, he demonstrates considerable awareness of audience (probably his teacher), whom he assumes has not seen these movies, and anticipates possible questions. Such rhetorical moves, I maintain, are first steps in acquiring school literacy. Notice, too, that movie plots themselves, not just movie watching, are inextricably woven into John's imaginative life, and it is that life, not his physical one, that makes up his "typical day."

Watching movies is a fixture in most students' lives, not just John's. Still, ethnic-based differences are evident in how students talk about movies. Significantly, these differences are the same differences in discursive practices evident in the students' other writings, including their personal and fictional narratives. For example, in his "Spring Break" paper, Collin, a white male student, explains that after working on the farm early in the week and buying a new camper, "that night our family watched the original 'Psycho' Hitchcock movie, that was a good movie but it was scary. Wednesday the day went much the same way. That night our family watched another Alfred Hitchcock movie: 'Rear Window'. That was a good movie also, it had one of my favorite actors in it, James Stewart."

Collin's movie synopses differ from John's in at least two major ways. First, the family's movie selections are critically acclaimed Hitchcock classics, shown in two consecutive evenings in a kind of home film festival before the family leaves for the rest of the week to go camping. These selections rightly suggest the educational level of the parents (Collin mentions elsewhere that his father is college educated); they also point to the status of mainstream movie classics in the household, which clearly hold middle-class aesthetic and intellectual values. Second and more important, Collin includes affective commentary not just about the movie but about "one of my favorite actors, James Stewart," which displays his knowledge beyond the immediate context of *Rear Window*. Thus Collin makes connections within the larger knowledge domain of cinema history.

In another paper entitled "My Favorite Movie" (apparently a make-up assignment or possibly an enrichment assignment because no other students wrote on this topic), Collin demonstrates his knowledge of books as well as of the movie review genre.

My Favorite Movie

One of my favorite movies I've seen lately is the "Lord of The Rings." It was really good. That kind of movie You have to like what it's about. The movie had Wizards, Orcs (goblins), Elves, Dwarves and things like that.

The movie is about a ring that controls all of the evil that has taken over middle-earth and can only be destroyed by throwing it into the fire where it was made.

The movie is also a book written by J.R.R. Tolkien. I've read "The Hobbit" and thats the prelude to the "Lord of the Rings" series. There are four books total and they go in this order. "The Hobbitt," "The Fellowship of the Ring," "The Two Towers," and finally, "The Return of the King." I tried quite a while ago to read the "Fellowship of the Ring," but it really thick and I didn't have time.

The movie I'm talking about is "The Fellowship of the Ring." The reason it's called "The Fellowship of the Ring" is because some characters get together to journey to Mt. Doom where the Ring was made so they can destroy it. The trip is very dangerous so some of the people making the journey are warriors. First theres' Frodo he is the ring bearer because he inherited it. And there is three other hobbits: Sam, Merry and Pippen. One Dwarf named Gimley goes along with them, one elf (and my favorite character) Legolas, two human warriors: Aragorn (aka Strider) and Boromir. And last is Gandalf the Grey, he is a wizard that aids them in their journey.

Throughout the whole movie there is constant action. The 9 journeyers are always fighting the Orcs. The movie is gorey but, not that bad for a PG-13 rating. If you haven't seen this movie yet I would recommend it to you.

In his opening paragraph, Collin implicitly identifies the genre (a movie with "Wizards, Orcs (goblines), Elves, Dwarves and things like that") as key to whether someone else would like this movie and follows through with a one-sentence paragraph that neatly dispenses the exposition, after the manner of a television schedule synopsis. After situating the movie within the larger context of the Tolkien series, he manages to explain the significance of the title and sum up the plot, again in one sentence ("The reason it's called 'The Fellowship of the Ring' is because some characters get together to journey to Mt. Doom where the Ring was made so they can destroy it."). Most of that paragraph, in fact, is devoted to identifying and categorizing the characters in order of importance and in relation to one another as well as to the plot. With an obvious awareness of diverse audiences, Collin closes with a mention of "constant action," an evaluative criterion important to his age group, and a disclaimer that the movie is rated PG-13 because it is gory but "not that bad," an evaluative criterion important to parents. This kind of telegraphic closing is typical of movie reviews in newspapers and other local news outlets, while the last sentence ("If you haven't seen this movie yet I would recommend it to you") is a classic book report closer through elementary and middle school levels (and sometimes beyond). Collin clearly liked the movie, but he conveys that message ironically by using "objective" analysis, not affective commentary.

Collin demonstrates more, however, than his internalized sense of a critical review, school book report, and other genres in the entertainment domain. He also demonstrates a certain kind of slice-and-dice thinking, one that can compress information; break it down to finite specificity (e.g., "four books . . . in this order"; "9 journeyers"); categorize it; recontextualize it; and so on. This is precisely the kind of thinking—usually called "critical thinking"—that is most valued in academic discourse. And it is the kind of discourse that runs almost exactly counter to the way students from Mexican-origin homes (especially, but certainly not exclusively) are socialized to use language. Literateness is a learned behavior, and as learned behavior is both cultural and epistemological at once. Heath (1991) sums up well how school success is predicated on a certain orientation to the world, one that coincides with Euro-American, middle-class values:

> A critical thinker . . . is an individualist, a reflective skeptic, a questioner, a doubter, an arguer, and an observing bystander. . . . But what promotes the integration of verbal display of knowledge with the critical stance in an individual? Clearly, those who perform critical thinking emerge most predictably only as a result of learning certain attitudes, language uses, and orientations toward social roles in early socialization practices. The primary sociocultural group in which such performers are born must value individualism; combative, information-based rhetoric exchanged among individuals; and acceptance of attention by participants to something more than their own immediate and direct sensory experiences. The social organization of the group must be more than open to change; it must value change as a phenomenon unto itself. (p. 12)

IMPLICATIONS FOR TEACHING

Bedtime story reading in Maintown homes, then, prepares children in multiple, reinforced ways for the kind of thinking, discourse practices, and interaction styles requisite for long-term school success. But story reading is a white, middle-class phenomenon, one that is foreign in most working-class homes of color. The English teaching profession generally has promoted certain home policies, such as reading 30 minutes every day, as key to improving students' reading comprehension as well as enlarging their frame of reference beyond personal experience. Home support for academic literacy is of course important. But recommendations such as reading 30 minutes every day fail to take into account the very real consequences of economic and cultural differences in the home lives of students of color.

What is needed is not home intervention, I maintain, but school intervention. I want to suggest that TV watching can potentially play as critical a role in children's sense of literateness in Rondo as story reading does in Maintown. In fact, because preteens and early teens across all ethnicities watch more television than any other age group (Buckingham, 1993), all students could benefit from an integration of television (and especially, movies) into the curriculum throughout the secondary level, in ways that the ensuing discussion will explore.

The buzz-phrase "culturally relevant curriculum" takes on new meaning in a rural, multiethnic community. Cultural relevance for young adults is contemporary popular culture—not traditional texts, songs, and the like. In the Rondo papers, students occasionally allude to the role of traditions in their lives, such as quinceañera (a Latina girl's 15th birthday celebration of her entrance into womanhood) and longhouse ceremonies (a longhouse is the site for the religious and community services for American Indians). In a community such as Rondo where religion is important, one would expect to see the influence of religious discourse in students' writing, and it does appear in the one assignment where such discourse would be most appropriate, the "What I Am Thankful For" assignment written at Thanksgiving.

Metonymy and parallelism abound in almost every paper produced for that assignment. One student writes, "I'm also thankful for having a roof over my head and a floor under my feet." Another student sustains the same parallel structure for three sentences before breaking from the pattern in the fourth, when she expresses her heartfelt thanks for TV: "I am thankfull for food because if we did not have food we would probably die. I am also thankfull to have school and if we did not have school everyone would be ignorant. Another thing that I am thankful for are my family members because if it was not for them, I would not be here. I am also thankful for my television because it intertanes me." TV makes it to the top of one student's list of necessities of life that are usually taken for granted: "I am thankful for T.V. hot water and electricity or I've would have been cold." But other discursive influences from traditional discourses are otherwise rare. In his personal narrative, one student explains "why we call Brian Blackfoot Brian Fatfoot," a line that bears resemblance to fables and traditional folktales about how animals came to have certain attributes. In her "Spring Break" paper, another student tells an Easter egg hunt story: "I looked in Lucky's house our little puppy it wasn't there. So

I looked on the table that my parents were siting by it wasn't there. So I looked under the trampoline because there was two balls to play with. I looked there and there was the egg." The writer plots her story on a cycle of three, not unlike a fairy tale—and not unlike many television cartoon plots. "I have traditions," another writes in his "All About Me" paper, "but I can't really remember." Such statements speak to the cost of assimilation: the loss of traditional culture in the lives of immigrant and American Indian families. But it is a loss that has not caused most of these students much pain, at least not yet. "On the way over there [to another state] my brother put on Spanish music, which I don't like, just to annoy me and my sister," one girl writes in her "Spring Break" paper.

Simply put, popular culture is the common culture of young adults across ethnic boundaries: "common" in the sense of being ordinary but also in the sense of being shared (Willis, 1990). Common culture inhabits their domestic spaces as well as their social practices (i.e., choices in clothes, music, magazines, romance rituals, banter, dance). All of this symbolic creativity surrounding young adults' appropriations of popular culture is not inconsequential. Further, these visual texts are among the most racist and sexist in everyday life outside of school. Analysis of their meanings and their meaning-making mechanisms needs to be included in every English language arts classroom. But how?

Using TV and movies in the secondary curriculum would not necessarily entail actually showing them in class. To a large degree, teachers can assume that these visual narratives constitute the common knowledge base for most teenagers. One study found that teenagers know about current movies in great detail, even when they themselves have not seen them— enough to participate in daily conversations where their peers share affective comment and even coperform "the good parts." Showing single scenes from select movies or asking students to work from movies that they have already seen or know about are solid alternatives to running up against school censorship. These materials can provide a base for a critical literacy curriculum on at least three levels.[10]

At the most obvious level, attention needs to be directed at issues of representation. For example, several Rondo students wrote that Jackie Chan movies generally and *Rush Hour II* specifically were their favorite movies. Why are these movies so funny, and to whom are they funny? Such a question should open up discussion on stereotypes, and beyond: What's the difference in using stereotypical characters, for example, in *Rush Hour II* and in *Dumb and Dumber*? How might different members of an audience view these stereotypes? In other words, what meanings do these movies, often by means of stereotypes but also by other means (i.e., casting, score, and film editing), create for different kinds of viewers, defined by race, class, gender, sexual orientation, and so forth? The point of such an inquiry is not, however, to condemn the movies or even racial and gender stereotypes. To do so depreciates the popular culture and devalues its importance in young adults' lives, which defeats the purpose of incorporating it into the secondary curriculum in the first place. That kind of discussion, so common in schools, merely serves the status quo, which privileges alphabetic literacy over visual, oral, and multimedia literacy. Young adults are, in fact, the most sophisticated readers of visual and multimedia images of any age group (Willis, 1990), so an equally sophisticated investigation of those images is well within their reach.

On a second level, students need to examine more subtle forms of representing bias. They need to be directed to explore what values are embedded in the visual narratives of movies and to what degree these values support or undermine their own. At this level, issues of meanings need to be recontextualized and critically framed in terms of the local as well as the national and global. Storytelling embodies not just the forms but also the norms of a community. Do the stories told by Hollywood serve the same social-oriented purposes of the family lore these students have heard all their lives? Do movies valorize human beings who survive humbly and miraculously? What orientations to the world, to the community, to individuals are embedded in these narratives? Besides making connections between their own collective stories and those of mainstream entertainment, they need to widen their gaze to other genres and media as well. Asking tough questions of literary materials as well as community resources, such as local and state newspapers, will help students see that the ultimate aim of learning to read is reading to learn. And reading to learn is more than merely collecting "objective" information, no matter if that information is dressed in literary or nonliterary clothing. Simply put, there is no such thing as a neutral and innocent text.

And finally, on a third level, the genres generated by the entertainment industry can be introduced into the classroom as a bridge to academic literacy. Comparing blurbs on a video box and a wide range of movie reviews written for different audiences and even in different media model different ways of handling the same kind of information. These particular forms are precisely applicable to fictional and nonfictional narrative, the genre that predominates in most language arts curricula. Such genre models abound, which students can emulate as they write about an art form that they know and care about. Most important of all, this kind of analysis typifies a certain kind of thinking prized in American education, where information is broken down, decontextualized and recontextualized, synthesized and evaluated.

Cultural relevance also takes on new meaning in a rural, multiethnic community that is quickly becoming immersed in electronic media, and not just television and movies. In their writing assignments, students reported daily use of various media, including telephone, cell phone, video games, TV, and computers. Many talk of playing video games on their Play Stations and Nintendo 64; and all of them report watching movies on their television sets. Many of those television sets are connected to cable, although most families rely heavily on renting or buying movies, rather than using cable, perhaps in efforts to make the most of their entertainment dollars.

And what of computers with Internet access at home? Eight students mention they have computers at home; what's more, they are allowed to use them apparently any time that they wish, except (ironically) during homework time. Three other students talk of going to someone else's house to use a computer, and another one says that he uses the computer daily to check his e-mail at the community center every day after school. One student writes in his "A Typical Day" paper that he goes home after school and will

> watch tv; if nothing on, then video games; when get bored, get on the Internet. I always chat with my friends and send messages to my relatives and my best buddies. At 7:00 am to 7:30 am I read my book. I try to finish a chapter or two before I stop reading my book. After Im done reading my book I go eat a snack. Then I go to sleep and turn on the radio so I could go to sleep faster.

Chat and e-mail are woven into the daily fabric of another student's life, as she points out in two different essays: "[After school] after I eat and do my homework I check my E-mail. Then I watch T.V. until dinner." "I got home and did my usual, got a snack and got on the internet." This same students uses her computer before school: After she wakes up, she turns on the radio, "then I put my make up on. After that I eat breakfast. Then I get on the computer, and chat on the internet in chat room. At about 7:00 am I go to school."

Of the eight students with home access, four of them use e-mail or chat; the other four only mention using their computers for playing games or for unspecified purposes. Quite possibly, the four of the eight students who talk about playing games on the computer were not connected to the Internet. Certainly, home Internet access is constrained by socioeconomic class, for connectivity minimally requires subscription to an Internet service provider, an ongoing expense that most families in this community can ill afford. Still, it is interesting to note that the four students who reported using e-mail and chat on a daily basis were white and Filipino.

Although this observation has no statistical validity whatsoever, I do want to suggest that perhaps ethnicity—and not just economics—influences how a family uses the home computer. The white and Filipino students report using e-mail and chat as solitary users on home computers not located in the central family room; the Latino students report playing games and listening to music with family members on home computers located in central living areas. Generally, media use is hugely affected by previous experiences with other media (Haas, 1999). In Rondo, TV watching time is family time and peer group time, and computer time seems to be spent in much the same way under similar circumstances, at least at this early stage of Internet penetration in Indian country. One student wrote of one incident where she, her younger sister, and grandmother all got on the same computer to play games. But this scene will probably not play out this way when these students are themselves grandmothers. Families can easily gather around a TV set; not so a computer monitor. Hardware design suggests that a solitary user will be writing on a keyboard, and only two or three users can comfortably sit and read a monitor.

However, traditional patterns of interaction, usually organized around gender and age for the Latino population in particular, will probably persist for several generations, and computer-assisted communication does not pose a threat to those patterns. Quite the contrary. Young adults talking with one another—whether online or off—is a culturally consistent pattern of interaction and learning for both Latino and American Indian students (Rhodes, 1994; see also Cajete, 1999; Calderon, 2001; Calderon & Carreon, 2001; Fashola, Slavin, Calderon, & Duran, 2001; B. Monroe, 2002). But young adults talking to one another *online* would afford them a new way of displaying knowledge, one that is more culturally consistent than public oral demonstration and individual pen-and-paper tests, the two means most common in public schools, especially high-poverty schools. Talking online with peers allows students to reflect before speaking, even if that pause is a momentary one as it is in chat sessions. This moment of reflection not only allows them to save face as a safeguard against public shaming, it also allows them to de-face—that is, not put themselves on public display and show off—because they are not lone speakers standing up in front of a listening, silent audience. And finally, online interaction will allow students to model not only written English as a code but also certain kinds of language use. American Indian and Latino students generally learn best from demonstration. Traditionally in both cultures, the teacher will demonstrate a task over and over, with minimal or no verbal explanation; the learner attempts the task when she believes she can complete it successfully (B. Monroe, 2002). Teachers, too, can model written English online as they interact with students in that environment. Clearly, Rondo students have not seen much written English, and learning through imitation and practice may be the best way for them to learn so-called basic skills.

The references made by the eight students with outside-school computer access says much about the growing influence of computers in the lives and literacies of Rondo's younger generation. Their reported daily use, too, suggests the potential impact of computer-mediated communication on their schooling—a potential that will never be realized without radical policy intervention at this point. Rondo Middle School teachers are required by the central administration to teach from the literature textbooks, even though most students are reading at about fourth grade level. In reading and writing alike, the emphasis is on basic skills. Even though the school has a fully equipped computer lab with 35 stations connected to the Internet, it is only used by students on academic probation to do the Accelerated Reader program (and a math program similarly designed to "drill and kill"). Thus, "the pedagogy of poverty" (Haberman, quoted in Nieto, 2002, p. 193) with its top-down, chalk-and-talk methods prevails in the computer classroom as well.

To be sure, all students need to work on their basic skills just as they need to learn to read for comprehension. But literacy education need not proceed in lockstep sequence, with students having to answer what-questions before why-questions and before giving affective commentary. Actually, just the reverse may be true; the more alienated the group of students, the more important it is to address the issues at the root of that alienation: the huge breach between home and school literateness (see also Garcia, 2001). Students need to know the ways of the "culture of power" (Delpit, 1988, p. 282)—to wit, that certain discursive practices as well as interactive styles derive from white, middle-class ways of thinking, talking, and writing, and these provide the bedrock patterns of discourse, interaction, and knowledge display required in school. Heightening this alienation from school is the working-class awareness that the kind of literate behaviors required in school will not be valued or even needed in the job sectors that await them: agriculture, ranching, and the trades. All the more reason to strive for a sense of critical literateness, one that works from the premise that for students of color, academic literacy is an instance of interethnic communication, and that they need to become bicultural in order to succeed in school. The lesson that literacy is epistemology is one that all students—not just students of color—need to learn in the English classroom.[11]

This awareness is an important antidote to the assimilationist agenda of public schools generally; otherwise, students of color will continue to drop out, or worse, they will stay in school and be at risk of losing confidence in their abilities or their drive or both. Differences in their own ways of seeing the world—differences in epistemologies—need to be explicitly drawn, and the comparison should not come at the expense of students' home literacies, too often described in terms of lack. Basic skills should be understood within this context also. We need to tell students that they have to master skills like punctuation and capitalization, not because these skills will necessarily improve their lot, but because they will further limit their choices if they do not. Consistent with the project of critical literacy, too, is a careful, critical consideration of popular culture's impact on young adults' literate lives. Popular culture is not just entertainment. It provides the mainstay of the imaginative lives of young adults. And it is a powerful tool of assimilation, for good and for ill.

Movies are their stories. As such, they need to be brought into the classroom in a systematic, critical way, along with other kinds of stories that represent the best (and the worst) that has been thought and written. There are all kinds of stories—canonical, popular, communal, personal— that keep people of color in their place on the reservation: in the fields and at the most menial jobs in a subsistence economy. Incorporating popular culture and computer-assisted communication in the classroom can burn paths between school and home, especially in ethnically diverse, impoverished communities just off the main highway.

CHAPTER 5

Revisiting the
Access Issue

In April 1997, a teacher at Detroit High School told me that the UM/
Detroit project had "transformed this school."

Detroit High School in 1997 certainly seemed much different from the
school I first visited in 1994. Students had written more in that year as a
direct result of the project than they had in all their previous school years
put together. Teachers printed out the UM tutors' online conferences and
shared them with their colleagues, discussing the priorities of those conferences and what those priorities say about what counts for "good writing"
in college—that is, within white mainstream culture. Before 1996, the creative writing teacher desktop-published a literary magazine of student writing on her home computer; after 1996, students produced the magazine
themselves at school. According to the school's assessment coordinator,
teachers became aware of how isolated they were when they participated
in the national ACT workshops that were part of the project. And according to the district's instructional technology team, students at Detroit High
School were the most computer-literate in the district. Before the project,
the school was one of the most isolated schools in Detroit; in the years
during and immediately after the project, the school welcomed a steady
stream of visitors—administrators, teachers, tech teams from across the
district and the state—who came to see their model computer classrooms.
What they saw there was not just the hum of fully operative computers but
also the hum of student activity, the sound of students focused and engaged. Enrollment spiked an extra hundred students from 1995 to 1996 to
an all-time high of 1,906. This spike was a direct result of the school's
high profile and newfound reputation for computer access, according to
the principal. And absenteeism decreased the year of the project, according
to teachers, because students wanted to work on computers.

These changes were substantive at the time. The sudden infusion of
technology created the initial chaos/opportunity and impetus for change,

115

as technology has done elsewhere at thousands of schools across the country. But were these changes transformative? That is, did they effect permanent, systemic change?

That information technology (IT) has transformative potential is generally taken for granted. According to an MCI poll in 1999, 60% of the public believe that IT could transform student learning. A special congressional commission, after assessing the success of the Clinton-Gore Technology Literacy Challenge, declared, "The question is no longer if the Internet can be used to transform learning in new and powerful ways. The Commission has found that it can. The issue before us now is how to make good on the Internet's promise for learning" ("Power of the Internet," 2000). That is the issue under consideration in this chapter. While previous research has identified major trends in IT use in schools generally, the case studies in this book flesh out these trends in nonwhite, high-poverty schools. "The local and the particular" (to recall Cynthia Selfe's phrase) can tell us to what degree transformation may be case-sensitive, for our case studies focus on schools and districts of different sizes, governance structures, missions, IT plans, and student populations—from voluntary to involuntary minorities, from minorities whose ancestors were kidnapped and enslaved to minorities whose ancestors were vanquished and almost exterminated. What these populations have in common, of course, is that they all reside on the other side of the digital divide.

That one factor, it turns out, outdistances all others in predetermining whether or not IT realizes its promise for learning. Updates on these four schools in 2003 will shed light on how the introduction of technology affected teaching and learning in these respective settings, not just in the short run, but over the long haul. Although the face and pace of change differed from school to school, these updates tell the same story: Change is only skin-deep without the technological resources and critical pedagogy to sustain it.

LOCAL UPDATES, 2003

The 35–work station Macintosh lab that originally served the UM/Detroit project now sits idle, worn out after years of use. The educational technician sits there all day with nothing to do, like the Maytag repairman, not because the machines do not need repair but because the machines are beyond repair.

The computers served the English Department well for five years. Then in 2001–02 the network was down more often than it was up; in 2002–03 it was down all year. Although almost all of the teachers involved in the original project have left, the remaining teachers are generally computer literate, thanks in large part to the district's laptop-for-teachers program. The teacher most involved in the UM/Detroit project regularly uses e-mail, but America Online is her Internet service provider, not the district's new e-mail system, a lesser known alternative. She routinely assigns writing, but more so when students are motivated and able than when they are not. It is just too hard, she explains. She estimates that roughly one-third of her students now word process their papers. Most of that one-third have home access; others seek out computers at the local university, the public library, community centers. Her students are resourceful, she says. The teacher also allows students making up assignments to send their work to her personal e-mail account. Even if the lab were refurbished, English teachers would have difficulty using it, for they are now spread out around the building, rather than concentrated in one wing. Moreover, the principal whose vision propelled the school forward into the Information Age in the mid-1990s has been moved to another part of town to a middle school.

This restructuring of personnel reflects a larger reality of Detroit Public Schools. In 2001 the district was privatized, red ink and low test scores leading to this loss of local control. The superintendent is now a CEO; students are clients and customers. The district's Web page projects its newfound corporate image, but does not reflect the realities evident at Detroit High School—to wit, the total and continuing lack of resources: paper, books, chalk, not to mention access to computers, much less the Internet. Yet, according to the district's Web page, chats can be scheduled through the central site, and tools are available for school Web site management and something called "TeacherNOTES/CIRCULARS for parents and students" ("Detroit Public Schools," 2003). This tool putatively has two-way capability: parents and students can download assignments, and they can communicate with teachers via e-mail within the tool as well. Technical support is centralized and available through e-mail and telephone. And perhaps most interesting of all, the site also endorses and links to tutor.com, a commercial one-to-one, online tutoring service. Individual students may seek out help on homework, or schools might contract with the service. If the Web site does not reflect current realities, perhaps it projects a vision for the future? According to one anonymous source inside the district, the Web page is "just window dressing" for the world. Although the corporation now running the district has spent millions of dollars on computers, Detroit High School, one of 268 schools in the district, has been allotted exactly none.

Garland High School, the Latino-majority school that was the focus of Chapter 3, presents yet another context for understanding how the access issue continues to play out in painfully predictable ways. Even though

Garland High School is larger than Detroit High School, its 2,400 students are served by only two computer labs equipped with 30–32 computers in each lab, although students often have to share because rarely are all the computers working. A third computer lab is reserved strictly for career research. The labs are located in the library, the annex (a good 10-minute walk from English classes), and the counseling area. Teachers must sign up to bring their classes to a lab generally 2 weeks in advance. Students have Internet stickers indicating that they have parental permission to use the Internet, and then only with teacher supervision. Each teacher has a computer in her classroom, which she uses for keeping grades, taking roll, and checking e-mail.

The teacher who implemented *The Crucible* project allows her students to use her classroom computer to type papers and to do occasional research, but large class sizes disallow more consistent use in instruction. Her classroom, like many in the building, has recently been wired with four Ethernet outlets for additional equipment in the future; how far in the future is not known. As much as she would like to continue doing inter-school exchanges like the one she did in 2000, additional curricular requirements occasioned by state mandates, as well as limited and inconvenient access, have forestalled integrating online projects on a regular basis. While the school struggles to keep pace with the computing needs of a large student population in a resource-poor district, students do have more access outside of school than they did back in 2000 when *The Crucible* project took place. Students who do not have a computer at home may go to a friend's or relative's house that does. Additionally, the school computer labs are open after school for several hours. These two access points—the school labs and someone's home access—have insured that most students, although certainly not all, are typing or composing their papers on computers for their classes.

The extra Ethernet hookups in the instructional spaces, as well as other signs, point to future directions envisioned by the district's IT planners. The district offers computer classes for parents—another indicator that the community as a whole is coming online. The IT department also offers several computing classes for students, such as 3-D animation and multimedia production of various kinds; the computers used for these classes, however, are off-limits for academic classes. While most teachers have desktop computers, many participate in a laptop-for-teachers program. However, these laptops are good mainly for word processing, because IT has removed most other programs. The IT department and teachers have not had good rapport historically.

The Garland district Web site, like Detroit's, seems to endorse more progressive computing practices than supported in the past. Besides the usual links to educational resources for both students and teachers, the site also links to Global SchoolNet, billed as the original clearinghouse for collaborative projects from across the globe. The Global SchoolNet site itself has a searchable database of teachers and projects, using a full range of communication technologies, to connect students in interschool collaborations and discussions. But the link to Global SchoolNet was dead when I accessed the old site in early 2003 as the district was putting up a new site; the Global SchoolNet link was dropped altogether when the new site came up later in the year.

And what of the 100-student Tribal School that partnered up with Garland High School for *The Crucible* discussion? The collaborating teacher left the following year to teach at a middle school in a public school district closer to her home. Although Tribal School lost this early adopter, the faculty started to learn computing themselves. With aid from a federal grant, the 10-member faculty each received a laptop; from there, they pursued a weekly, in-house professional development program. They sent select faculty to workshops, and they brought in a teacher trainer from a nearby school. Tribal School in 2003 has several computers in every instructional space, although most are not networked and few run off the same operating system—the result of hand-me-downs and small, sporadic purchases. Still, the teachers are making good use of their laptops, gradually expanding their use from word processing to browsing, searching, presenting in PowerPoint, and e-mailing. They are bringing these uses to the classroom and learning just ahead of (and sometimes, along with) their students.

The IT picture at Rondo in 2003 is not as bright. The teacher who participated in the project discussed in Chapter 4 left the district the following year. As may be recalled, her students collectively wrote almost 800 papers in the course of that school year, 2001–02. Only a few students word processed their work from their home or community center. Even though a new computer lab with 35 stations was located about 50 feet from the classroom door, these students were not allowed to use it. The lab was reserved solely for Accelerated Reader and Accelerated Math, a series of stand-alone CD-ROMs that the district uses for its credit-retrieval program for at-risk students. That situation remained unchanged in 2003.

FROM "TRANSFORM" TO "REFORM"

These four schools bring home the national trends in IT use over the past decade. On the Garland district Web site, the dead link to, and then the disappearance of, Global SchoolNet nutshells the regressive trajectory of

IT from the 1990s to the 2000s. As Garland goes, so goes the nation. Talk of "transforming" education, prevalent in the 1990s, has given way to talk of "reforming" education in the 2000s. In effect, IT revolution has been co-opted and now largely serves the status quo, especially in high-poverty schools. In each case, we see the introduction of computers disrupting the status quo and initially transforming classroom practices. In three of the schools, we see that early excitement dissipate and many of the teaching gains lost as the schools were either unable to keep up with demand (at Garland High School) or unable to sustain computing resources (at Detroit High School) or disallowed open access to teachers and students (at Rondo Middle School). Tribal School, the last of these schools to come online and still in the introduction stage, will most likely have similar difficulty in maintaining current resources.

Many studies have noted that IT has not lived up to its early hype. Oddly enough, these studies are based on schools in high-SES communities. The situation is even more extreme in low-SES schools, and not just because of a lack of resources, a point I will return to in just a moment. Larry Cuban (2001) found that schools in the Silicon Valley were generally well-equipped, but that computers were underutilized and remained peripheral to instruction: 40% used computers for word processing, and another 40% did not use computers at all, especially at the secondary level. Another study, which released eight reports called the Teaching, Learning, and Computing (TLC) reports, surveyed 2,250 teachers in grades 4–12, in public and private schools designated technology-rich and specifically dedicated to educational transformation as an outcome. Even in these hothouse conditions, the TLC researchers found that teachers tend to use IT—if they use it at all—to support their current teaching beliefs and practices (Becker, Ravitz, & Wong, 1999).

Notably, those beliefs differ in high-SES and low-SES schools, according to the TLC reports. Teachers in low-SES schools are more likely to favor traditional classroom practices and are more likely to see computers' potential for equipment damage and cheating than are teachers in high-SES schools. They are more likely to have their students use computers for routine drills than to make presentations, do analytical work, or write. They are less likely to assign homework that requires computers. And they are very clear on why their students should use computers: to develop job market skills (Becker et al., 1999). The lack of cognitive challenge and low skill level of these computing tasks, however, will only prepare these students for the lowest paying jobs where obedience, not critical literacy, are requisite.

In contrast, high-using teachers in high-SES communities say their objectives for high-achieving students are to present information and communicate with other people. Such activities, teachers say, engage students enough that they tend to use computers outside of class, at home or before or after school (Becker et al., 1999). This frequency and kind of IT use prepare these high-achieving students in high-SES communities to assume managerial and entrepreneurial livelihoods in their future (Warschauer, 1999). The differences in kinds of use in low- and high-SES classrooms may be directly attributable to home access. Both students and teachers in low-SES communities are less likely to be able to afford computers at home. Further, these schools would have less money for teacher training and technical support (Becker et al., 1999; Becker & Riel, 2000; Ravitz, Becker, & Wong, 2000).

But money does not tell the whole story. For these class-marked differences in IT use are further exacerbated by the high-stakes testing movement. Teachers in low-SES schools are under more pressure than their counterparts in high-SES schools to focus on basic skills at the expense of more cognitively challenging curriculum. Often mandated to "teach to the test" by administrators, they resort to traditional practices to transmit more efficiently this basic-skills knowledge (Becker et al., 1999; Becker & Riel, 2000; Ravitz et al., 2000). The principle that instructional goals should drive the technology, not the other way around, is one that is repeated, like a mantra, at technology workshops for teachers. And it is good advice, depending on what those goals are. For instructional priorities are inextricably tied to the SES, and implicitly the race and ethnicity, of the community a school serves.

Those priorities favor traditional teaching practices, which support de facto race-based tracking practices. Such tracking patterns may be evident within a single institution or entire districts. For example, Mark Warschauer (1999) noted in his study of one class at a Christian college whose mission is to prepare future missionaries, but apparently in very racial-ethnic–specific ways: Asian students in the English as a Second Language class used computers primarily to drill and word process their assignments for the instructor's eyes only, thus implicitly teaching them to obey orders from above. School districts at extreme ends of the socioeconomic scale tend to adopt one track or another as their mission. Historically, high-poverty schools of color have in fact been more restrictive and authoritarian than other school settings, in large part because of their basic-skills instructional priorities, but also because of their assimilationist agendas (Cuban, 1993; Goodlad, 1984; Sizer, 1984; Street, 1995). Thus test scores drive the curriculum as well as instructional priorities and teaching practices at most high-poverty schools because low scores shape public perception and threaten local control of schooling. Indeed, Detroit Public Schools has already been taken over by the state and subcontracted out to a private corporation. Even Tribal School was placed in "corrective action" in 2002 by the Bureau of Indian Affairs, meaning that they have 7 years to improve student learning, as measured by test scores, or be shut down.

In fall 1999, after reviewing the goals of the Clinton-Gore Technology Literacy Challenge, the U.S. Department of Education found those goals largely achieved and declared the need for a new national educational technology plan for the next decade. This new strategic plan calls for students and teachers to have access in their classrooms, schools, communities, and homes, in hopes that these multiple access points "will help end the isolation of teachers; exponentially expand the resources for teaching and learning in schools and classrooms; provide more challenging, authentic and higher-order learning experiences for students; and make schools and teachers more accountable to parents and communities" (U.S. Department of Education, 2001). The plan also calls for content and networked applications that "will support transformative changes in our approaches to teaching and learning." But the overarching point of this new national IT plan is to use "technology as a tool to improve academic achievement" ("Enhancing Education," 2001).

I want to suggest that the new national plan is at cross-purposes if academic achievement is measured solely by high-stakes tests. These tests are grounded in white, middle-class literacies and take the form of white ways of learning through individual competitive display. In high-needs schools where other Englishes, literacies, and learning preferences prevail, test scores will always be low, and therefore basic skills, not critical literacy, will continue to be given instructional priority. In support of this priority, computers will be used predominately for drills and multiple-choice quizzes, if at all, in order to save time by way of direct transmission instruction. In an era of high-stakes testing, then, while some teachers may individually pursue innovative IT use and critical literacy goals, the transformative promise of IT will not translate systemically into transformative practice.

TAKING ACTION NOW

How does systemic change happen? The short answer: from the bottom-up. The new federal Congressional Commission acknowledges the importance of grassroots teacher involvement at all stages of a school's IT implementation plan: "The Commission saw first-hand the policies that most influence technology use in education derive from bottom-up, interconnected grassroots efforts far more than from top-down dictates" ("Power of the Internet," 2000). Other studies have found that IT implementation is most successful when teachers develop a collective plan for their departments and buildings. Collaborating on this local plan also creates opportunity for ongoing collaboration on curriculum and methods; according to the TLC reports, teachers who keep their classroom doors open are the ones most likely to experiment with and share innovative methods. Notice that at Garland High School and Rondo Middle Schools, teachers have no say whatsoever in ground-floor decision making; they are not even informed that new facilities are being installed. The same might be said of Detroit High School, only worse: teachers are not informed of IT plans for the district, but those plans do not include them anyway. Tribal School, however, is a different story. The faculty make the decisions about all of the school's social, academic, and economic concerns. They operate from a consensual model of governance that has its ancient roots in tribal culture, a model that holds that everyone must agree on solutions and courses of action because everyone needs to play a role in those solutions and courses of action.

Equal access across the digital divide will always be illusory, as long as the power and poverty differential that undergirds it exists. That differential will not disappear in our lifetimes. In the meantime, teachers in high-poverty schools can act now by transforming their own classroom practices, even if school access is limited or even nil. In high-SES communities where schools are most likely to have access in labs and in the classroom, students do not want to use computers at school, preferring to use their own home computers. Increasingly, teachers in these schools expect students to use this home access, assigning everything from research papers to video projects, all to be done outside the school day. In low-SES communities where schools do not provide or allow access, students are nonetheless finding other means to connect. A 2003 report notes that teenagers are spending more time using computers than watching television. Compared to 2001 figures, home Internet use among minority and low-income teenagers has surged, and more than two-thirds of low-income households have home access ("Study: 'Digital divide' shrinks," 2003). According to the teachers involved in our four case studies, students rely on friends and relatives who share their private resources; they also seek out alternative sites of access, such as community centers and public libraries. Somehow, increasingly, these students are coming to school computer literate (and visually literate, to boot). As the Detroit teacher said, "They're resourceful."

To teachers in high-poverty schools I say, challenge your students to use these out-of-school sites of access, bearing in mind certain traditional practices will have to be tossed. Not everyone needs to be using the same medium, doing the same assignment, all the time. Encourage students to word process their work. Provide them with the intellectual and technical framework for posting papers online through Listservs, participating in on-line threaded discussions, and using Web-based e-mail to message their peers to seek and offer help. I stress the communication technologies—e-mail and online threaded discussions—because they allow student-to-student communication, within and between classes or schools and univer-sities. Yet, even word processing, which admittedly has its own hidden imperialism (McGee & Ericsson, 2002), can become a radical pedagogy—even a political act—in a school like Rondo, which has a computer lab but neither teachers nor students have a say in how it is used. Word processing could help these students learn the vagaries of the written language; more important, students would need to be able to think critically about those red and green squiggly lines inserted by spelling and grammar checkers, questioning their appropriateness and authority within the immediate con-text of their own writing. In short, connect their worlds with the world of school, using the tools and topics that dominate their lives.

Nor is this advice a matter of "let them eat cake." If many, even most, cannot find access, English teachers can still use paper and peers in trans-formative ways. Even without any technology, we should make all writing public writing, available for modeling and oral performance, peer-to-peer. And whether our students have access or not, instructional goals should remain the same as for students in high-SES schools: to wit, critical literacy, which is prerequisite for social action. These demonstrable pedagogical needs, in turn, will put pressure on the system to accommodate those needs. In other words, show; don't tell. Show administrators that IT can be used in transformative ways. And show them, too, that there is indeed a pressing need for Internet access. Until all students have home access, public points of access need to developed and expanded, especially in high-poverty schools. If we are using IT in transformative ways, access will need to be available both within and outside the classroom as well as during, before, and after the school day. Further, we need to work collectively to make the case at district levels that, in a decade of shrinking budgets, the poorest schools with the lowest test scores—not the magnate schools, not the rich-est ones—should be the first to get computers, not the last (if ever).

IT, in and of itself, is no magic wand, even if high-poverty schools did magically, suddenly have adequate access for all students. But IT and criti-cal pedagogy together can transform schools on the other side of the divide in ways not really possible using any other means. Besides opening up channels between "haves" and "have-nots" and between different groups of "have-nots," IT can transform top-down, teacher-centered practices, which currently favor white ways of knowing and learning. As I have shown, individualistic, competitive displays of knowledge run counter to Latino, American Indian, and African American values. Learning peer-to-peer and learning by demonstration and modeling are more characteristic of these traditional, honor-shame cultures. Further, the Internet opens up new channels of expression, allowing one to see "increasing salience of cultural and linguistic diversity" (Cope & Kalantzis, 2000, p. 5), which includes both traditional and situational variations in the language.

And finally, linguistic diversification of the Internet might in the very, very long run transform standards, or at least transform the talk about standards. Racist assumptions about language use will not go away until the public—not just teachers—is aware that other Englishes, other rhetorics, and indeed, other epistemologies do exist. From there we can talk about how to honor the home literacies that students of color bring to school, even as we teach all children, not just children of color, to become interethnically literate.

Notes

CHAPTER 1

1. The first NTIA report in 1995 only mentions the Internet once in the text of the report and once in a footnote to that place in the text. At that point in time, apparently, the Internet was still irrelevant as a market force.

2. *Wired* covers featured African Americans only two other times in the 1990s: first, in September 1995, O. J. Simpson, digitally whitened (and a blackened Nicole Brown Simpson inside); and second, in December 1994, images apparently in connection with the story "Gang War in Cyberspace," a lengthy account of the hacker gang war between the Legion of Doom and the Masters of Deception. I say "apparently" because both hacker gangs were actually comprised of blue-collar white males, with only one African American member among the six major players in this early cyberwar. For a discussion of the O. J. Simpson images in *Wired*, see Warnick, 2002.

3. I give full credit to Greg Hooks, Professor of Sociology at Washington State University, for this argument.

CHAPTER 2

1. In brief, the project did not accomplish its expressed goal—to create a new admissions pool for recruiting well-prepared and fully funded African American students to the University of Michigan. Further, the project was supposed to continue for 3 years after students were connected, but in fact only lasted a little more than one calendar year. Changes in administration at all levels at the University of Michigan rescinded the university's long-standing commitment to academic outreach and redirected those resources to on-campus initiatives.

2. For an in-depth analysis of that emergent genre that we were using at this point in time, see "The Look and Feel of an OWL Conference" (B. Monroe, 1998).

3. I draw all of these figures from information given to me at the time from various sources. Most came from district personnel as we collaborated in writing up our proposal to respective stakeholders in the UM/Detroit project. In subsequent news releases about the project, however, the principal insisted that the official

poverty figures for the school and the area not be included. She did not want the appearance of, in her words, "poor-mouthing." This protectiveness of Detroit's image accounts in part for the city's small-town feel, I believe. From that uncommon sense of community, however, comes Detroit's much-storied xenophobia. Outsiders are always viewed with suspicion until they prove that they "walk the walk" as well as "talk the talk," an adage that I heard many times in the 3 years I worked with the school. As a side note, in the mid-1990s the Crips and the Bloods had not successfully established themselves in Detroit because they were viewed as outsiders: Even gangs honor the insider-outsider divide evident in so many areas of Detroit life.

4. Although I am drawing mainly from Kochman's work in this section, I am reformulating his chapter on personal disclosure. I have also folded in several other well-established observations about African American expressive culture from another chapter in Kochman's book, the chapter on bragging and boasting, as well as from cultural anthropologists and from my own work and observations.

5. Coupled with a clowning performance in sports, this event is called, variously, *grandstanding*, *showboating*, or *hotdogging*. When this behavior is deemed "taunting," it becomes a rule violation in many college and professional sports. These speech events are not instances of self-aggrandizement; they aim to entertain and maintain a community through laughter that bonds as well as releases the tension of competition. In playing the role of the clown, the performer is directing laughter not at the opponent but to himself or herself.

6. Of course, topical appropriateness varies from culture to culture and has long been an important consideration in contrastive rhetoric. One of the founders of that field of inquiry, Robert Kaplan pointed out at a guest lecture at Washington State University in 2000 that North Americans do not like to talk about death and bathroom functions, whereas in Thailand it is customary to ask, "Did you have a good bowel movement this morning?"

7. A version of this assignment can be found in Rick Monroe's *Writing and Thinking with Computers* (1993).

8. For all the citations from the electronic record, I have taken great care to copy and paste passages as they were written by both UM tutors and Detroit students. I have not inserted "[sic]" for the sake of readability.

9. Sociolinguists and cultural anthropologists, such as Baugh (1983), Abrahams (1976), and Hymes (1974), prefer the term *style-shifting* over *code-switching* to designate shifting between SAE and AAE. Baugh rightly points out that the switch is not really an instance of code-switching because the two varieties of English are mutually intelligible, whereas switching from Spanish to English, for example, is clearly an example of switching to another language code. Still, I use *code-switching* specifically to mean switching between SAE and AAE, which would include the distinctive grammatical, phonological, and lexical features of the two varieties of English, because I want to underscore the fact that the two are distinct, mutually legitimate varieties of English. I use *style-shifting* more inclusively to mean the rhetorical shifts characteristic of the African American expressive tradition, with or without the aid of AAE. This rhetorical dimension takes into

account stylistic alterations occasioned by audience and context, precisely the parameters I want to focus on in this discussion. *Style-shifting* should suggest to nonspecialists, too, that such shifts are matters of stylistic choice and verbal agility, not error and deficit.

10. AAE has many varieties, and Detroit AAE is one of the most distinctive of those varieties phonologically. While the phonology of Detroit AAE did not participate in the Northern Cities Shift as did other varieties in AAE in the North (Labov, 1998; Anderson, 2002), it has undergone significant change since the 1960s and now sounds similar to southern Anglo varieties. Anderson (2002) convincingly argues that the unique development and maintenance of Detroit AAE help maintain an ethnolinguistic urban identity unique to its inner-city residents. Detroit AAE is also class-marked to a certain degree. Baugh (1983) and Rickford (1999) maintain that socioeconomic status significantly affects use of AAE, as does context. I follow Baugh's analytical framework to explain the Detroit students' use of AAE; that is, its use is relative to insider-outsider status of the speaker and listener and relative to social domain.

11. In-group boundaries, in fact, are more often erected by language than by skin color; even minor differences in speech and gesture style often define group affiliations (Giles & Johnson, 1981).

12. During private auditions for the annual talent show, several students did perform "clean" raps. Although they were allowed to audition these raps as simply self-authored poetry, none made the final cut for the show. As the sponsor of the talent show explained to me, the school did not allow public performances of rap poetry.

13. I am not sure that the teacher's assessment of the situation was accurate, for Reuben's paper indicates that his grandfather showed him how to repair a tire, and he describes certain procedures with knowledgeable detail (e.g., how to test the tire by pumping it up first and then submerging it in a tub of water to see where air bubbles escape).

14. The similarity between some southern varieties of English and AAE has been variously explained. Dillard (1972) convincingly argues that the roots of AAE can be traced to a West African pidgin, which became creolized when Africans were brought to the New World and enslaved. As contact with other varieties of English increased for these speakers, especially in the twentieth century, the process of decreolization, or moving toward the standard, stabilized AAE as the distinct variety it is today. Southern varieties of "white" English have much in common with AAE, according to Dillard, because African American women in slave times often cared for white children along with their own.

15. The story behind David Schaafsma's title, *Eating on the Street (1994)*, neatly dramatizes this point. The African American teachers that Schaafsma was working with in a summer workshop in Detroit were mortified that their students decided to eat their snacks on the way as they walked to a downtown museum. "Eating on the street," in the teachers' phrase, made the whole community look bad. From their perspective, every individual must be on best behavior especially in public, for the actions of one reflects on the image of all.

CHAPTER 3

1. This information I gleaned from the U.S. Census, 2000, and from the Garland teacher's master's degree report. I have not cited either source, only in an effort to protect the anonymity of the schools.

2. I have not corrected students' typography, in part to capture students' idiom and skills level, but in larger part, to challenge the reader to look beyond the issue of basic skills to students' critical literacy. For the sake of readability, I have not inserted "[*sic*]" to indicate errors in the original.

CHAPTER 4

1. See also Baghban (1984), Bissex (1980), D. Butler (1975), Crago and Crago (1983), Herrnstein Smith (1978), Ninio and Bruner (1976), Taylor (1983), Taylor and Dorsey-Gaines (1988), Teale and Sulzby (1986), and White (1954).

2. Just as the students do in their writing, I use the phrases "TV watching" and "watching TV" to mean both watching television programs and watching movies on television sets. I use the word "movie(s)" to include all formats—VHS, DVD, cable, and satellite—as well as those shown in theaters.

3. I discuss the language socialization of Latino and white students in this chapter, but not that of the Plateau Indian and Filipino students. Although the Plateau Indian students' accounts of their home lives do not stand out as substantially different from those of their Latino counterparts, their rhetoric is clearly marked as distinctive. Thus I have included analysis of their narrative rhetoric but not of their language socialization at home. Analysis of the Filipino students' writing and language socialization I have omitted altogether, mainly because the sample was too small to make substantial claims and because it closely resembled the writing consistently produced by white students.

4. Exact population figures have been deliberately omitted to protect the anonymity of the town and ultimately of the human subjects involved in this research project. All of the figures about Rondo are taken from the U.S. Census Bureau report, 2000, although the interpretation of the data is my own. All percentages are rounded off for the sake of readability.

5. I derived the ethnicity of students' homes from several factors. Students self-identified their ethnic backgrounds on a questionnaire and in an autobiographical assignment at the beginning of the year. However, students often noted on their questionnaires all their biological ancestry, without noting what percent or how recent. Therefore, I made more definitive determinations based on (a) languages other than English spoken in the home (including Spanish, Plateau Indian, and Filipino-Tagalog) and (b) direct references in student essays to culture-specific activities, such as attending a quinceañera (a birthday celebration for a 15-year-old Latina girl) or ceremonies at the longhouse (the site of American Indian religious practice), usually indicative of cultural group affiliation. For students of more than one race, I determined only the two most dominant ethnicities that met most of

these same criteria: self-identified ethnicity in the questionnaire or essays; languages spoken in the home; and direct references to culture-specific activities. When I explicitly designate a student's ethnicity in this chapter, I always note the more dominant influence first. My main goal in making these designations is to determine what cultural influences are most prominent in the home lives of these students, and by implication, the interactive and communications styles that they have most likely been acculturated to.

6. Here and throughout the chapter, I have transcribed students' words exactly as they appeared on paper. Therefore, grammatical and mechanical errors that occur were in the original. I have not marked errors with "[sic]" because such insertions will further hinder readability.

7. Another possible reading of Jeff's remark is that it is a veiled political point about the loss of thousands of miles of salmon runs when dams were built to supply water for irrigation to support agriculture. For Indian nations, the loss was more than environmental; it was at once economic and spiritual. Fishing is absolutely central to the Indian way of life in the region.

8. These averages do not accurately measure the time spent watching TV. Some students said they watched TV all the time; another reported that she watched TV for 420 hours a week; yet another, just 20 minutes a week. I averaged the numbers as the students reported them on the questionnaire, omitting the numbers that were obviously impossible or indeterminate.

9. The titles are obviously just the ones they most recently watched, rather than their all-time favorites. According to Buckingham (1993), it is a common practice among preteens and teenagers to talk about the most recent as their favorite. Keeping up with the movies is a status marker for this age group, and this shared knowledge gives occasion for conarration. These conarrations are not chronologically retellings of the plot but an evaluative and performative process whereby adolescents select out "the good parts" to replay together.

10. The pedagogical approach I outline here is more theoretical than practical. To get practical application of my approach, see the archive of instructional units at http://www.wsu.edu/currents, which represent the best work done in my methods class using this approach. For lesson plans on using popular music in critical pedagogy, see Cope & Kalantzis, 2000.

11. Montero-Smith uses the phrase "epistemological imperialism" to explain the low achievement of students of color (2001, p. 332).

References

Abrahams, R. D. (1976). *Talking black*. Rowley, MA: Newbury House.

Anderson, A. B., & Stokes, S. J. (1984). Social and institutional influences on the development and practice of literacy. In H. Goelman, A. A. Oberg, & F. Smith (Eds.), *Awakening to literacy* (pp. 24–37). Portsmouth, NH: Heinemann.

Anderson, B. (2002). Dialect leveling and /ai/ monophthongization among African American Detroiters. *Journal of Sociolinguistics, 6*(1), 86–98.

Applebaum, S. (1999, September 27). Facing the digital divide. Cablevision. Retrieved February 25, 2002, from http://www.findarticles.com/m0DGC/6_24/59493555/p1/article.jhtml

Aronowitz, S., & Giroux, H. A. (1993). *Education still under siege* (2nd ed.). Westport, CT: Bergin & Garvey.

Aycock, A., & Buchignani, N. (1995). The e-mail murders: Reflections on "dead" letters. In S. G. Jones (Ed.), *Cybersociety: Computer-mediated communications and community* (pp. 184–231). Thousand Oaks, CA: Sage.

Baghban, M. (1984). *Our daughter learns to read and write*. Newark, DE: International Reading Association.

Balester, V. (1993). *Cultural divide: A study of African-American college-level writers*. Portsmouth, NH: Heinemann.

Ball, A. (1992). Cultural preference and the expository writing of African-American adolescents. *Written Communication 9*(4), 501–532.

Baugh, J. (1983). *Black street speech: Its history, structure, and survival*. Austin: University of Texas Press.

Becker, H. J., & Riel, M. M. (2000, December). *Teacher professional engagement and constructivist-compatible computer use*. Teaching, Learning, and Computing: 1998 national survey, report #7. Irvine, CA: Center for Research on Information Technology and Organizations.

Becker, H. J., Ravitz, J. L., & Wong, Y.T. (1999, November). *Teacher and teacher-directed student use of computers and software*. Teaching, Learning, and Computing: 1998 national survey, report #3. Irvine, CA: Center for Research on Information Technology and Organizations.

Berst, J. (2000, April 18). Why Clinton is all wet about the Digital Divide. ZDNet. Retrieved October 19, 2003, from: http://reviews-zdnet.com.com/4520-6033_16-4204422.html

Bissex, G. (1980). *Gnys at wrk: A child learns to write and read*. Cambridge, MA: Harvard University Press.

Brady, M. (2000, August 4). The digital divide myth. *E-Commerce Times*. Retrieved February 25, 2002, from: http://www.ecommercetimes.com/perl/story/3953.html

Bridging the digital divide. (1999, October 14). BBC News. Retrieved September 23, 2002, from: http://news.bbc.co.uk/2/hi/special_report/1999/10/99/information_rich_information_poor/466651.stm

Brown, C. (1987). Appendix: Literacy in 30 hours: Paulo Freire's process in northeast Brazil. In I. Shor (Ed.), *Freire for the classroom: A sourcebook for liberatory teaching* (pp. 215–231). Portsmouth, NH: Boynton/Cook.

Buckingham, D. (1993). *Children talking television: The making of television literacy*. London: Falmer Press.

Burbules, N., & Callister, T. (2000). *Watch it: The risks and promises of information technologies for education*. Boulder, CO: Westview Press.

Butler, D. (1975). *Cushla and her books*. Boston: Horn Book.

Butler, W. (1992). *The social construction of knowledge in an electronic discourse community*. Unpublished doctoral dissertation, University of Texas, Austin.

Cajete, G. (1999). The native American learner and bicultural science. In K. Swisher & J. Tippeconnic (Eds.), *Next steps: Research and practice to advance Indian education* (pp. 135–160). Charleston, WV: Appalachia Educational Laboratory.

Calderon, M. (2001). Curricula and methodologies used to teach Spanish-speaking limited English proficient students. In M. Calderon & R. E. Slavin (Eds.), *Effective programs for Latino students* (pp. 251–306). Mahwah, NJ: Lawrence Erlbaum.

Calderon, M., & Carreon, A. (2001). A two-way bilingual program: Promise, practice, and precautions. In M. Calderon & R. E. Slavin (Eds.), *Effective programs for Latino students* (pp. 125–170). Mahwah, NJ: Lawrence Erlbaum.

Chuck 45. (2001, February 2). Chairman Mike and the digital divide. *The Gully*. Retrieved February 25, 2002, from: http://www.thegully.com/essays/US/politics_2001/010212powell_fcc.html

Cochran, J. (2000, April 17). The digital divide narrows. ABCNews.com. Retrieved February 25, 2002, from: http://www.abcnews.go.com/onair/CloserLook/wnt000417_CL_digitaldivide_feature.html

Compaine, B. M. (2001a). Information gaps: Myth or reality? In B. M. Compaine (Ed.), *The digital divide: Facing a crisis or creating a myth?* (pp. 105–118). Cambridge, MA: MIT Press.

Compaine, B. (2001b). Preface. In B. M. Compaine (Ed.), *The digital divide: Facing a crisis or creating a myth?* (xi–xvi). Cambridge, MA: MIT Press.

Conley, D. (1999). *Being black, living in the red*. Berkeley: University of California Press.

Cope, B., & Kalantzis, M. (2000). A multiliteracies pedagogy: A pedagogical supplement. In M. Kalantzis & B. Cope (Eds.), *Multiliteracies: Literacy learning and the design of social futures* (pp. 3–8). London: Routledge.

Crago, M., & Crago, H. (1983). *Prelude to literacy: A preschool child's encounter with picture and story.* Carbondale: Southern Illinois University Press.

Cuban, L. (1986). *Teachers and machines: The classroom use of technology since 1920.* New York: Teachers College Press.

Cuban, L. (1993). *How teachers taught: Constancy and change in American classrooms 1890–1990* (2nd ed.). New York: Teachers College Press.

Cuban, L. (2001). *Oversold and underused: Computers in the classroom.* Cambridge, MA: Harvard University Press.

Delgado-Gaitan, C. (1990). *Literacy for empowerment: The role of parents in children's education.* New York: Falmer Press.

Delpit, L. (1988). The silenced dialogue: Power and pedagogy in educating other people's children. *Harvard Educational Review 58*(3), 280–298.

Detroit Public Schools. (2003). Retrieved April 20, 2003, from: http://www. detroit.k12.mi.us/

"Digital divide": About the series. (2000). PBS.org. Retrieved February 25, 2002, from: http://www.pbs.org/digitaldivide/about.html#series

Dillard, J. L. (1972). *Black English: Its history and usage in the United States.* New York: Random House.

Dyson, A. H. (1993). *The social worlds of children: Learning to write in an urban primary school.* New York: Teachers College Press.

Dyson, A. H. (1997). *Writing superheroes: Contemporary childhood, popular culture, and classroom literacy.* New York: Teachers College Press.

Dyson, A. H., & Genishi, C. (1994). Introduction. In A. H. Dyson & C. Genishi (Eds.), *The need for story: Cultural diversity in classroom and community* (pp. 1–7). Urbana, IL: National Council of Teachers of English.

Eldred, J. C., & Fortune, R. (1992). Exploring the implications of metaphors for computer networks and hypermedia. In G. E. Hawisher & P. LeBlanc (Eds.), *Re-imagining computers and composition: Teaching and research in the virtual age* (pp. 58–80). Portsmouth, NH: Boynton/Cook Heinemann.

Enhancing Education Through Technology Act of 2001. (2001, August). U.S. Department of Education. Retrieved October 19, 2003, from: http://www.ed.gov/ policy/elsec/leg/esea02/pg34.html?exp=0

Entwisle, D., Alexander, K., & Olson, L. (1997). *Children, schools and inequality.* Boulder, CO: Westview Press.

Faigley, L. (1992). *Fragments of rationality: Postmodernity and the subject of composition.* Pittsburgh, PA: University of Pittsburgh Press.

Faigley, L. (1999). Beyond imagination: The Internet and global digital literacy. In G. E. Hawisher & C. L. Selfe (Eds.), *Passions, pedagogies, and 21st century technologies* (pp. 129–139). Logan, UT: Utah State University Press.

Fashola, O. S., Slavin, R. E., Calderon, M., & Duran, R. (2001). Effective programs for Latino students in elementary and middle school. In M. Calderon & R. E. Slavin (Eds.), *Effective programs for Latino students* (pp. 1–66). Mahwah, NJ: Lawrence Erlbaum.

Feenberg, A. (1991). *Critical theory of technology.* New York: Oxford University Press.

Fox, H. (2001). *"When race breaks out": Conversations about race and racism in college classrooms.* New York: Peter Lang.

Freire, P. (1998). *The pedagogy of freedom* (P. Clarke, Trans.). Lanham, MD: Rowman & Littlefield.

Garcia, G. N. (2001). The factors that place Latino children and youth at risk of educational failure. In M. Calderon & R. E. Slavin (Eds.), *Effective programs for Latino students* (pp. 307–330). Mahwah, NJ: Lawrence Erlbaum.

Gates, H. L., Jr. (1990, July 15). The case of 2 Live Crew tells much about the American psyche [Letter to the editor]. *New York Times*, p. IV18.

Gearan, A. (2000, April 17). Government, industry to announce plans for bridging the digital divide. ABCnews.com. Retrieved February 25, 2002, from: http://www.abcnews.go.com/sections/tech/DailyNews/navaj0000417.html

Gee, J. P. (1990). *Social linguistics and literacies: Ideology in discourses.* Brighton, UK: Falmer Press.

Giles, H., & Johnson, P. (1981). The role of language in ethnic group relations. In J. C. Turner & H. Giles (Eds.), *Intergroup behaviour* (pp. 199–243). Oxford: Blackwell.

Goodlad, J. (1984). *A place called school.* New York: McGraw-Hill.

Graff, H. J. (1979). *The literacy myth: Cultural integration and social structure in the nineteenth-century city.* New Brunswick, NJ: Transaction.

Graff, H. J. (2001). The nineteenth-century origins of our times. In E. Cushman, E. R. Kintgen, B. M. Kroll, & M. Rose (Eds.), *Literacy: A critical sourcebook* (pp. 211–233). Boston: Bedford/St. Martin's.

Gravill, J. (1998). Utopic visions, the technopoor, and public access: Writing technologies in a community literacy program. *Computers and Composition* 15(3), 297–315.

Green, L. (2002). *African American English: A linguistic introduction.* Cambridge, UK: University Press.

Gruber, S. (1995). Re: ways we contribute: Students, instructors, and pedagogies in the computer-mediated writing classroom. *Computers and Composition* 12(1), 61–78.

Guinier, L. (1998). *Lift every voice: Turning a civil rights setback into a new vision of social justice.* New York: Simon & Schuster.

Haas, C. (1999). On the relationship between old and new technologies. *Computers and Composition* 16(2), 209–228.

Hacker, K. (2000). *Digital divide facts and fictions.* Retrieved February 25, 2002, from: http://khacker2.freeyellow.com/ddnow6.htm

Heath, S. B. (with Thomas, C.). (1984). The achievement of preschool literacy for mother and child. In H. Goelman, A. A. Oberg, & F. Smith (Eds.), *Awakening to literacy* (pp. 51–72). Portsmouth, NH: Heinemann.

Heath, S. B. (1986). What no bedtime story means: Narrative skills at home and school. In B. B. Schieffelin & E. Ochs (Eds.), *Language socialization across cultures* (pp. 97–127). Cambridge, UK: Cambridge University Press.

Heath, S. B. (1989). The learner as cultural member. In M. L. Rice & R. Schiefelbusch (Eds.), *The teachability of language* (pp. 333–349). Baltimore: Paul H. Brookes.

Heath, S. B. (1990). The children of Trackton's children: Spoken and written language in social change. In J. W. Stigler, R. A. Shweder, & G. Herdt (Eds.), *Cultural psychology: Essays on comparative human development* (pp. 496–519). Cambridge, UK: Cambridge University Press.

Heath, S. B. (1991). The sense of being literate: Historical and cross-cultural features. In R. Barr, M. L. Kamil, & P. B. Mosenthalpp (Eds.), *Handbook of reading research, Vol. 2* (pp. 3–25). Mahwah, NJ: Lawrence Erlbaum.

Henrickson, W. W. (1991). A shrinking city. In W. W. Henrickson (Ed.), *Detroit perspectives: Crossroads and turning points* (pp. 539–542). Detroit, MI: Wayne State University Press.

Herrnstein, R. J., & Murray, C. (1994). *The bell curve: Intelligence and class structure in American life.* New York: Free Press.

Herrnstein Smith, B. (1978). Children at the gates of the marketplace. In B. Herrnstein Smith (Ed.), *On the margins of discourse. The relation of literature to language* (pp. 124–132). Chicago: University of Chicago Press.

Holmes, S. (2000, September 27). Incomes up and poverty is down, data show. *New York Times*, p. A12.

Hooks, G., & Blair-Loy, M. (2000). *Race, wealth, and education.* Unpublished research proposal.

Hubbard, L. (2000, March 2). Is the digital divide a black thing? Salon.com. Retrieved February 25, 2002, from: http://www.salon.com/news/feature/2000/03/02/digital/index.html

Hudson, B. (2001). *African American female speech communities: Varieties of talk.* Westport, CT: Bergin & Garvey.

Hunn, E. S. (1990). *Nch'I-wana ("the big river"): Mid-Columbia Indians and their land.* Seattle: University of Washington.

Hurston, Z. N. (1935). *Mules and men.* New York: Harper Perennial.

Hymes, D. (1974). *Foundations in sociolinguists: An ethnographic approach.* Philadelphia: University of Pennsylvania Press.

Judge, P. (2000, March 2). A lesson in computer literacy from India's poorest kids. *BusinessWeek Online.* Retrieved October 4, 2002, from: http://www.businessweek.com/bwdaily/dnflash/mar2000/nf00302b.htm

Kaplan, R. B. (1966). Cultural thought patterns in intercultural education. *Language Learning 16*(1&2), 1–20.

Kochman, T. (1981). *Black and white styles in conflict.* Chicago: University of Chicago Press.

Kozol, J. (1991.) *Savage inequities.* New York: Crown.

Labov, W. (1998). Co-existent systems in African-American vernacular English. In S. S. Mufwene, J. R. Rickford, G. Bailey, & J. Baugh (Eds.), *African-American English: Structure, history, and use* (pp. 100–153). London: Routledge.

Lohr, S. (1996, October 16). A nation ponders its growing digital divide. *New York Times*, D5.

Mahiri, J. (1998). *Shooting for excellence: African American and youth culture in new century schools.* Urbana, IL: National Council of Teachers of English.

Marks, A. (2000, January 25). Digital divide narrows: Minorities closing high-tech gap. ABCNews. Retrieved February 25, 2002, from: http://www.abcnews.go. com/sections/tech/DailyNews/csm_divide000126.html

Marriott, M. (2000, October 18). Technology briefing: Hardware: 3Com rolls out an Internet appliance. *New York Times*, p. C8.

McGee, T., & Ericsson, P. (2002). The politics of the program: MS Word as the invisible grammarian. *Computers and Composition 19*(4), 453–470.

Media Education Foundation. (1995). *Democracy in a different voice with Lani Guinier* [videotape]. North Hampton, MA: Media Education Foundation.

Mehan, H. (1979). *Learning lessons*. Cambridge, MA: Harvard University Press.

Miller, P. J., Hoogstra, L., Mintz, J., Fung, H., & Williams, K. (1994). Narrative practices: Their role in socialization and self-construction. In U. Neisser & R. Fivush (Eds.), *The remembering self: Construction and accuracy in the self-narrative* (pp. 158–179). New York: Cambridge University Press.

Miller, P. J., & Mehler, R. A. (1994). The power of personal storytelling in families and kindergartens. In A. H. Dyson & C. Genishi (Eds.), *The need for story: Cultural diversity in classroom and community* (pp. 38–54). Urbana, IL: National Council of Teachers of English.

Monroe, B. (1994). Courtship, comedy, and African-American expressive culture in Zora Neale Hurston's fiction. In G. Finney (Ed.), *Look who's laughing: Studies in comedy and gender* (pp. 173–188). New York: Gordon & Breach.

Monroe, B. (1998). The look and feel of the OWL conference. In E. Hobson (Ed.), *Wiring the writing center* (pp. 3–24). Salt Lake: Utah State University Press.

Monroe, B. (2002). The Internet in Indian country. *Computers and Composition 19*(3), 285–296.

Monroe, R. (1993). *Writing and thinking with computers: A practical and progressive approach*. Urbana, IL: National Council of Teachers of English.

Montero-Smith, M. (with Batt, M. C.) (2001). An overview of the educational models used to explain the academic achievement of Latino students: Implications for research and policies into the new millennium. In M. Calderon & R. E. Slavin (Eds.), *Effective programs for Latino students* (pp. 331–368). Mahwah, NJ: Lawrence Erlbaum.

Moran, C., & Selfe, C. (1999). Teaching English across the technology/wealth gap. *English Journal, 88*(6), 48–54.

Morgan, M. (1998). More than a mood or an attitude: Discourse and verbal genres in African-American culture. In S. Mufwene, J. Rickford, G. Bailey, & J. Baugh (Eds.), *African-American English: Structure, history, and use* (pp. 251–281). London: Routledge.

National Telecommunications and Information Administration (NTIA). (1995, July). *Falling through the net: A survey of the "have nots" in rural and urban America*. Retrieved February 25, 2002, from: http://www.ntia.doc.gov/ntiahome/fallingthru.html

National Telecommunications and Information Administration (NTIA). (1998, July). *Falling through the net: New data on the digital divide*. Retrieved February 25, 2002, from: http://www.ntia.doc.gov/ntiahome/net2/

National Telecommunications and Information Administration (NTIA). (1999,

July). *Falling through the net: Defining the digital divide.* Retrieved February 25, 2002, from: http://www.ntia.doc.gov/ntiahome/fttn99/contents.html

National Telecommunications and Information Administration (NTIA). (2000, October). *Falling through the net: Toward digital inclusion.* Retrieved February 25, 2002, from: http://www.ntia.doc.gov/ntiahome/fttn00/contents00.html

Nichols, J. (1998, July 29). The digital divide. *Wired News.* Retrieved February 25, 2002, from: http://www.wired.com/news/politics/0,1283,14069,00.html

Ninio, A., & Bruner, J. (1976). The achievement and antecedents of labeling. *Journal of Child Language 5,* 1–15.

Novak, T. P., & Hoffman, D. L. (1998). Bridging the digital divide: The impact of race on computer access and Internet use. eLab Manuscripts. Retrieved October 19, 2003, from: http://elab.vanderbilt.edu/research/papers/html/manuscripts/race/science.html

Ohmann, R. (1985). Literacy, technology, and monopoly capital. *College English 47(7),* 675–689.

Oliver, M., & Shapiro, T. (1995). *Black wealth/white wealth.* New York: Routledge.

Online content for low-income and underserved Americans: The digital divide's new frontier. (2000). The Children's Partnership. Retrieved February 25, 2002, from: http://www.childrenspartnership.org/pub/low_income/index.html

Oppenheimer, T. (2000, Feb. 2). Greedy clicks. Salon.com. Retrieved February 25, 2002, from: http://www.salon.com/news/feature/2000/02/02/digital/

Porter, J. (1998). *Rhetorical ethics and Internetworked writing.* Greenwich, CT: Ablex.

The power of the Internet for learning: Moving from promise to practice. Web-based Education Commission. (2000). Retrieved April 27, 2003, from: http://interact.hpcnet.org/webcommission/index.htm

Pratt, M. L. (1991). Arts of the contact zone. *Profession 91,* 33–40.

Ratliff, E. (1999). Net free for all. *Wired.* Retrieved February 25, 2002, from: http://www.wired.com/wired/archive/7.12/mustread.html?pg=2

Ravitz, J. L., Becker, H. J., & Wong Y. T. (2000, July). *Constructivist-compatible beliefs and practices among U.S. teachers.* Teaching, Learning, and Computing: 1998 national survey, report #4. Irvine: Center for Research on Information Technology and Organizations.

Rhodes, R. (1994). *Nurturing learning in Native American students.* Hotevilla, AZ: Sonwai Books.

Rickford, J. (1999). *African American vernacular English: Features, evolution, educational implications.* Malden, MA: Blackwell.

Romero, S. (2000, October 2). Tribes seeking phone systems as step to Web. *New York Times,* pp. A1, A25.

Schaafsma, D. (1994). *Eating on the street.* Pittsburgh, PA: University of Pittsburgh Press.

Schroeder, C., Fox, H., & Bizzell, P. (2002). *ALT DIS: Alternative discourses and the academy.* Portsmouth, NH: Heinemann.

Selfe, C. L. (1999). *Technology and literacy in the twenty-first century: The importance of paying attention.* Carbondale IL: Southern Illinois University Press.

Selfe, C. L., & Selfe, R. J. (1994). The politics of the interface: Power and its exercise in electronic contact zones. *College Composition and Communication* 45(4), 480–504.

Shaughnessy, M. (1977). *Errors and expectations: A guide for the teacher of basic writing*. New York: Oxford University Press.

Sinclair, J., & Coulthard, M. (1975). *Towards an analysis of discourse: The English used by teachers and pupils*. New York: Oxford University Press.

Sites aim for African Americans. (1997, September 17). C/net News.com. Retrieved February 25, 2002, from: http://news.cnet.com/news/0-1005-200-316646. html?tag=rltdnws)

Sizer, T. (1984). *Horace's compromise: The dilemma of the American high school*. Boston, MA: Houghton Mifflin.

Sloan, S. (1999). Postmodernist looks at the body electric: E-mail, female, and hijra. In K. Blair & P. Takayoshi (Eds.), *Feminist cyberscapes: Mapping gendered academic spaces* (pp. 41–61). Stamford, CT: Ablex.

Small-town broadband allure. (2000, December 4). ISP-Planet. Retrieved October 19, 2003, from: http://www.isp-planet.com/politics/ars_policy.html

Smitherman, G. (1977). *Talkin and testifyin: The language of black America*. Detroit, MI: Wayne State University Press.

Steele-Carlin, S. (2000). *Caught in the digital divide. Education world*. Retrieved February 25, 2002, from: http://www.education-world.com/a_tech/tech041. shtml

Street, B. (1995). *Social literacies: Critical approaches to literacy in development, ethnography, and education*. London: Longman.

Study: "Digital divide" shrinks among U.S. kids. (2003, March 20). Retrieved April 18, 2003, from: http://www.cnn.com/2003/TECH/internet/03/20/digital.divide. reut/

Sugrue, T. J. (1996). *The origins of the urban crisis: Race and inequality in postwar Detroit*. Princeton, NJ: Princeton University Press.

Tannen, D. (1981). Indirectness in discourse: Ethnicity as conversational style. *Discourse Processes* 4, 221–238.

Tannen, D. (1990). *You just don't understand: Women and men in conversation*. New York: Ballantine Books.

Taylor, D. (1983). *Family literacy: Young children learning to read and write*. Exeter, NH: Heinemann Educational Books.

Taylor, D., & Dorsey-Gaines, C. (1988). *Growing up literate: Learning from inner-city families*. Portsmouth, NH: Heinemann.

Teale, W., & Sulzby, E. (1986). *Emergent literacy: Writing and reading*. Norwood, NJ: Ablex.

Titone, J. (2000, December 25). Flexing too much muscle? *The Spokesman-Review*, pp. A1, A10.

Toy, V. S. (1994, December 21). $100-million will be used to create jobs and rebuild neighborhoods in empowerment zones. *The Detroit News*, pp. 1A, 11–12A.

Turner, J. C., & Giles, H. (1981). Introduction: The social psychology of intergroup behaviour. In J. C. Turner & H. Giles (Eds.), *Intergroup behaviour* (pp. 1–32). Oxford: Blackwell.

Ulrich, R. (1999). *Empty nets: Indians, dams, and the Columbia River.* Corvalis: Oregon State University Press.

U.S. Department of Education. (2001, January). *E-learning: Putting a world-class education at the fingertips of all children.* Washington, DC: Author.

Villanueva, V. (1993). *Bootstraps: From an American academic of color.* Urbana, IL: National Council of Teachers of English.

Walker, F. (2003). An Afrocentric rhetorical analysis of Johnnie Cochran's closing argument in the O. J. Simpson trial. In R. Jackson & E. Richardson (Eds.), *Understanding African American rhetoric: Classical origins to contemporary innovations* (pp. 245–262). New York: Routledge.

Warnick, B. (2002). *Critical literacy in a digital era: Technology, rhetoric, and the public interest.* Mahwah, NJ: Lawrence Erlbaum.

Warschauer, M. (1999). *Electronic literacies: Language, culture, and power in on-line education.* Mahwah, NJ: Lawrence Erlbaum.

Warshauer, S. C. (1995). Rethinking teacher authority to counteract homophobic prejudice in the networked classroom: A model of teacher response and overview of classroom methods. *Computers and Composition 12*(1), 97–112.

Welsh, S. (2001). Resistance theory and illegitimate reproduction. *College Composition and Communication 52*(4), 574–611.

White, D. (1954). *Books before five.* Portsmouth, NH: Heinemann.

Willis, P. (1990). *Common culture: Symbolic work at play in the everyday cultures of the young.* Boulder, CO: Westview Press.

Wolf, S. A., & Heath, S. B. (1992). *The braid of literature: Children's worlds of reading.* Cambridge, MA: Harvard University Press.

Index

About the Author

Barbara Monroe started teaching in the Houston area in 1969 in a white, working-class community that was home to dockworkers and the Imperial Grand Wizard of the Ku Klux Klan. It was there that she learned the abiding lesson that has informed her lifework: The goal of a good English education should be critical literacy, not just literacy.

Since then, she has taught at all levels, pre-K through college, here and aboard. After teaching in the public school classroom for 10 years, she taught Mexican migrant workers at night and Libyan oilmen by day. A nontraditional student herself, she received her degrees in three different decades, receiving her PhD from the University of Texas at Austin in 1992. Migrating from Austin Community College to the University of Michigan, she worked in alternative programs for so-called underprepared students, who were, not coincidentally, predominantly students of color or working-class students or both.

She has implemented school-university partnerships, first with the Detroit public school system and later with reservation schools in the Pacific Northwest. Barbara is currently coordinator of English education at Washington State University, where she continues, coyotelike, to crisscross boundaries—institutional, disciplinary, and cultural. Few working in the field today have had her wide-ranging experience with high-poverty populations with different racial majorities in different regions of the United States.